JULIUS CAESAR

BOOKS BY MANUEL KOMROFF

JULIUS CAESAR

MARCO POLO

NAPOLEON

JULIUS CAESAR

by Manuel Komroff

JULIAN MESSNER, INC., *New York*

Published by Julian Messner, Inc.

8 West 40th Street, New York 18

Published simultaneously in Canada

by The Copp Clark Company, Ltd.

Copyright 1955 by Manuel Komroff

Printed in the United States of America

Library of Congress Catalog Card No. 55-9859

JULIUS CAESAR

chapter
one

Julius Caesar, the greatest of all Roman soldiers and statesmen, was born in 100 B.C. He belonged to one of the oldest and most distinguished families of Rome, a family that traced its ancestry back to Aeneas, the mortal son of the goddess Venus.

It was Aeneas who at the fall of Troy was ordered by the gods to sail across the seas until he reached the distant shores of a mysterious land which we now know as Italy. Here, it was decreed, he was to settle and lay the first beginnings of the Roman Empire. And it was from this famous man that all the Caesars were descended. Julius Caesar was named after the god Julius, who was the son of Aeneas.

Caesar was an only child and although his mother and father were rich, he was brought up in a modest way. The other boys of his time and class knew every luxury of Rome—rich clothing, jewels, exotic foods and endless amusements. But this was not true of the young

Caesar. From his earliest days he was trained in the simplest ways and manners. Even his education was different from that of other boys.

Most Roman boys were educated by Greek slaves whom their parents bought as tutors. But Caesar's father and his mother, Aurelia, wanted Caesar to be educated by a freeman and so they engaged a gentle scholar named Gnipho as his teacher. This man was a Gaul and came from northern Italy. And it was under his care that Caesar, as a very small child, learned not only the prescribed Latin, Greek, history, literature and mathematics, but also the language and ways of the people of Gaul. From his gentle teacher, Caesar first heard about the origins of the Gauls, about their Druid priests and about their lands which stretched beyond the Alps. But as he listened with wonder to the strange stories which Gnipho told him, he had no way of knowing that one day he would be a great general and conquer this distant land and add its vast regions to the great Roman Empire.

The child Caesar loved to have Gnipho tell him stories of Gaul, but he also loved to hear the story of Rome, the little city built on seven hills which had grown so great that it was now master of the entire civilized world.

He often asked his tutor, "Tell me again about the Seven Kings and about Hannibal and the barbarian hordes."

And Gnipho would then relate the wondrous story of the rise of Rome. "Long, long ago, in its earliest days, Rome was ruled by Seven Kings. But the people tired of their rulers and dreamed of governing themselves. And so, four hundred years ago, they rose up and over-

threw the monarchy and established a democratic government, the same Roman Republic under which we live
today. From that time to this, the people of Rome have
ruled themselves."

Then Gnipho would go on to tell how the little walled
city rose to be the greatest power in all the civilized
world of its time.

"The people of Rome were happy with their new
government and hoped for peace. But the tribes which
inhabited the Italian peninsula, and which had at times
been set upon and conquered by the Seven Kings, now
began to attack her. Luckily, however, they did not join
forces; they fought Rome separately and so, one by one,
Rome was able to conquer them until she controlled the
whole of Italy from the Alps south to the very tip of
the boot. These lands became the first Roman provinces.
However, this conquest was not accomplished quickly;
it took a full two hundred years. And during this time
Rome suffered an attack from the north which has not
been forgotten to this very day. Great hordes of fierce
men from the dark forests and lands of a distant country
called Germany pushed down through Gaul, the land of
my people, and into Italy. They had long flowing hair
and beards and were dressed in animal skins. The glance
of their eyes was so wild that they struck terror into all
who saw them. And they did not have an organized army
like Rome has today, but traveled in great masses—men,
women and children together with horses and whatever
cattle they owned or could steal. They sacked and burned
Rome and then they went back to their own lands. And
after they were gone the people of Rome looked upon
their city in despair. It had been so devastated that there

were some who wanted to abandon the site and build a new city somewhere else. But in the end it was decided to rebuild Rome on its seven hills. And so the new city rose from the ashes of the old."

Gnipho then told the child the story of the long war with Carthage, a war which lasted off and on for over sixty years. He told how Carthage, a great city on the North African coast, had watched Rome conquer Italy, how she had begun to fear Rome and to look upon her as a rival and how she determined to destroy her. And so she declared war. Rome did not fall during this long war, however; instead she grew into a mighty military power. In order to protect herself and her Italian provinces, she was forced to build a great army and fleet, and to become a military power. In order to protect the shores of Italy from attacks she found it necessary to conquer neighboring lands such as Illyria on the far side of the Adriatic Sea and the islands of Sicily, Sardinia and Corsica.

"But it was Hannibal, the young general from Carthage," said Gnipho, "who brought the horrors of war home to Italy. He was only twenty-eight but he was brave and fearless. Since he felt that the war would never end unless Carthage could capture Rome, he led a great army of infantry, cavalry and elephants through Spain, along the Mediterranean shore of southern Gaul and over the Alps into Italy! He did what no other man had ever done before. He led his forces through the high snowbound, ice-covered passes of the Alps. Many of his men and elephants perished from the cold and hardships or lost their footing and crashed to their deaths from the mountain precipices. But Hannibal was not discouraged and when his men grumbled he spurred them on by pointing out to them the distant sunlit lands of Italy to the south. This, he said, was soon to be theirs!"

This was the part of Rome's story which the child Caesar knew almost by heart. The brave young Hannibal fired his imagination. The thought of a whole army of dark-skinned men from North Africa, leading their great elephants over the snowy Alps, filled him with wonder and awe. "And Hannibal succeeded in what he had planned to do," added the child. "He invaded the whole of Italy, didn't he?"

"Ah, yes, he did," replied Gnipho. "He swept over the entire land burning and pillaging, but he never conquered Rome. He remained in Italy for fifteen long years, but the Romans and Italians had by this time built such powerful armies that Hannibal never knew a moment's peace. And the coveted prize, the city of Rome, never fell into his hands. As a matter of fact, he was finally forced to abandon Italy and rush back to Carthage to try to save the city of his birth from destruction.

"A young Roman general named Scipio first sailed an army across to Spain and conquered that land from Carthage. Then he carried his forces across the Mediterranean to destroy the proud city of Carthage itself. The city fell. But even after this Rome did not know peace," continued Gnipho. "New enemies arose and the Roman armies traveled far and wide, conquering as they went. Macedonia and Greece became Roman provinces. Western and southern Asia Minor, far across the Aegean Sea, signed binding treaties of friendship. And Syria and Egypt also became Rome's allies. It was in this way that the Roman Empire first came into being. But before the armies could once more return home to Rome, they had to attack Carthage a second time. She had once more grown strong and Rome feared she would again cause trouble."

"Yes," interrupted the child Caesar. "Scipio led our armies back to Carthage and laid siege. For five whole years the city held out. But then it finally surrendered and all the inhabitants were killed or sold into slavery and it was burned to the ground. And then by special order of our Senate here in Rome, the land on which Carthage had once stood was plowed up and sown with salt and a curse was laid upon any man who should try to rebuilt it !"

It was in this way that the young child Caesar learned the past history of Rome. And when he was twelve years old civil war broke out in the city and he then saw history being made.

A Roman general named Sulla marched an army into Rome and took possession of the city, and for the first time the child Caesar saw soldiers patrolling the streets. And within his home he heard his parents and their friends speaking in whispers of strange things, frightening things. They said that certain people were being hunted out like beasts and dragged from their homes and killed. They said that the government, the Republic which had first been founded four hundred years before, had been brushed aside and Sulla had said that the Senate, the house of the aristocrats, was to rule instead of the people.

But far worse than all this to little Caesar was the fact that his uncle Marius had been forced to flee to distant Africa to escape being killed ! His uncle Marius who had led brave Roman legions in North Africa. Later he had taken them across the Alps into Gaul, where no Roman army had ever gone before, to drive back the German barbarians who were once more threatening Italy. And when the boy asked his parents and Gnipho why all these things were happening, he learned for the first time that the people of Rome and Italy were divided amongst themselves and that great suffering and misery existed.

"You are rich and have everything you need," said his father," but most of the people are poor and homeless. They do not have enough food to eat and no houses in which to live. Naturally they complain, but Sulla who sides with the rich and powerful senators has brought his army into the city and stilled their grumblings by killing all the men who sided with them. That is why your uncle Marius had to go away. He is the leader of the people. He is the head of the Popular party."

Then Caesar's father went on to say that many years ago, before Rome had begun her conquest of foreign lands, life had been very different. The rich had not owned great houses in the city and estates with rambling villas in the country. They had lived in a more modest way. And the whole of Italy had been divided into small farms owned and tilled by peasants and their families. There had been very few slaves and the rich had not been very rich and the poor very poor.

"But with the growth of the Empire all this changed," he said. "Great wealth and thousands upon thousands of slaves poured into Rome. And those who belonged to the aristocratic class and had money and power became richer and more powerful. They bought up the small farms of Italy and manned them with slaves. In a few years almost all the land was owned by a few rich men and the thousands of peasants were homeless. They crowded into the cities, especially Rome. And here they and their children have lived, generation after generation, in horrid poverty and misery, unable to find work or to buy food to eat. . . . They are forced to live in slums. They cannot find work because they cannot compete against slavery; some slaves sell for as little as one dollar on the slave block. The state gives them a dole of cheap grain to keep them from starving. The army is their only refuge. But when the fighting is over they are thrown back into the city's streets without reward. Only the rich get the spoils of war. And so the people ask that the land be given back to them. And those who live in other cities and towns also complain. They no longer want to be ruled by Rome unless they are allowed to vote. But the aristocrats who sit in the Senate, and men like Sulla, do not want to give up what they hold and so now they have taken the government by force and plan to rule exactly as they choose."

Then Caesar's father told him that although the Caesar family was one of the oldest and most important families throughout all Roman history, its members had seldom sided with the other aristocratic families. "Our family," he said proudly, "has always thought first of Rome and the welfare of all the people. We have not tried to win wealth and power through the misery of others. Through the centuries many members of our house have won glory fighting for democratic ideas. Your uncle Marius, who is married to my sister Julia, is today the foremost leader of the people and we are all proud that he married into our family."

Thus it was that the boy Caesar first heard of the

troubles which tore at the very heart of his country. But soon Sulla and his troops left for the far-off shores of Asia Minor and his uncle Marius returned and restored the old government. He and another popular leader named Cinna were elected consuls, or heads of the government, by the grateful people. And they passed many reforms, the most important of which was that the vote was given to all Italians without reserve or qualification. This included all those who lived south of the river Po. The lands north of this river were not considered Italian soil; they were called Cisalpine Gaul which means "Gaul south of the Alps."

For the next few years Rome lived in peace and young Caesar spent his days happily studying with his tutor Gnipho, and playing with his friends, among which was a boy named Marcus Cicero. They attended the public baths where they spent many hours and went to the arenas to watch gladiators in combat and chariot races. They wandered through the Forum and listened to political orations. They went to parties and sometimes they rode out into the country to visit the rich villas of friends. Here they swam in pools or in the ocean, played games and raced horses.

Although these were, for the most part, carefree days for young Caesar, three important events occurred in his life at this time. When he was fourteen, his uncle Marius, who was then consul appointed Caesar as priest of Jupiter and member of the Sacred College. Marius did this in order to honor the Caesar family, and since the child was directly related to the gods it seemed a fitting act.

The boy was greatly pleased, but the joy which he felt was soon dispelled when his uncle suddenly died.

Then two years later when he was sixteen his father also died. This added a second sorrow to his life. From this time on he turned to Aurelia, his mother, for advice and friendship. Aurelia was a woman of great wisdom and strong character. She came from an old and distinguished family. And through the years that followed she devoted herself completely to the interests of her only child. For the next thirty years she lived and watched his career with anxiety and pride.

chapter

two

The years of peace which Rome had enjoyed under the consulships of Marius and Cinna and the rule of the Popular party now suddenly came to an end. Sulla, having completed a brilliant but bloody campaign in Asia Minor, unexpectedly landed with forty thousand troops at Brindisi on the heel of the Italian boot and started a march on Rome. He was determined to wreak revenge against the people and the Popular party for the overthrow of the government he and his friends of the senatorial class had established.

Sulla's march on Rome was, however, not an easy one. It took him an entire year. He was forced to fight for every mile of the way. The provinces through which he passed were hostile and joined with the government forces under Cinna, which had come out to fight him. In time, nevertheless, Sulla was completely victorious and he entered Rome with his army.

Sulla was at once proclaimed dictator by his friends

in the Senate. He knew that nine tenths of the people hated him and his aristocratic friends but he did not care. He had complete contempt for the people and liked only those of wealth and birth. And with power once more in his hands he at once set about to strip the Popular party of its leaders. He instituted a Reign of Terror. He did not limit himself to Rome but ordered that lists be drawn up all over Italy of those who had ever supported the Popular party. Since a bounty of twenty-five hundred dollars was offered for every head and each informer was promised half of the victim's confiscated property, many idle and desolate people joined in the hunt. They roamed the streets of Rome and throughout the countryside seeking victims.

Almost five thousand people died at this time. There were no trials and no pardons. Suspicion was considered sufficient evidence. And Sulla's aim was completely realized; the Popular party was wiped out and he and his senatorial friends took complete control of the country. The people no longer had a voice in their government; they were allowed to retain their vote but they were never given a chance to use it.

It was after all these things had taken place that Sulla turned his attention to a personal matter. There was a young man in Rome who had escaped the Terror. He was twenty years old and, although he had as yet taken no part in the political scene, he came from a family which was well known for its Popular sympathies. Besides, when he was seventeen he had fallen in love with and married Cornelia, the daughter of Cinna. His name was therefore definitely joined to the Popular cause. And Sulla felt that unless he could be won over to the senatorial side he might someday become a leader of the people. His name was Julius Caesar.

These were the thoughts which filled Sulla's mind concerning Caesar. But before the young man could be taken into Sulla's group he would, of course, have to divorce his wife. And so Sulla summoned Caesar and ordered him to divorce Cornelia and marry another young woman whom he had picked out for him.

But young Caesar defied the all-powerful Sulla! He loved Cornelia and Julia, the little daughter who had been born to them, and he would not allow his home to be torn asunder. He answered boldly, "As long as I live I shall be my own master—master of all matters which concern me. Cornelia is my wife and she shall remain my wife as long as she lives."

Sulla was infuriated at the insolence of the young man. How dared he defy him! Yet, wanting to use young Caesar's family name and prestige, he did not at this time order him to be killed. He first tried to break his obstinacy. He stripped Caesar of his priesthood. Then he confiscated Cornelia's dowry and the estate Caesar had inherited from his father. And it was only after these measures had failed to bring the young man to reason that he secretly put a price upon his head and ordered his daggermen to seek him out.

But Caesar had friends in all parts of Rome and he was warned in time. Disguising himself, he fled into the mountains in the dead of night, where he hid in a cave.

However, it was not long before Caesar's hiding place was discovered. Two thugs arrived at night. But before they had a chance to do their work Caesar cleverly engaged them in conversation and won them over. He first complimented them on having found him. He said that it was not an easy thing that they had accomplished for his hide-out was well concealed; besides, he had not told anyone where he was going.

The rude assassins were pleased to be thought clever. They smiled.

"And what is more," added Caesar, "You are fortunate. Very fortunate. You do not know how fortunate."

The men did not understand.

"But you are being fooled."

"How?" asked one.

"The price which you are being offered for my head is not enough."

"Why not?"

"Because my head is worth ten times the amount you have been promised."

"Ten times!"

"Yes."

"But who would pay ten times the amount?"

"Not Sulla," answered Caesar. "But I know someone who would."

"Ten times?" repeated one.

"Yes."

Then the other assassin added, "With ten times the reward money we could be rich and we could live like gentlemen. But who would ever pay us such a sum for a single head?"

"I would," replied Caesar.

"You?"

"Of course. The head that you are looking at is worth more to me than it is to anyone else. Besides, I don't like to see you cheated."

"But the money. How will we get it?"

"I will give it to you."

"Now?"

"No. Not now, because here in the mountains I have no gold. But in Rome...."

"Oh, you cannot go back to Rome," the two warned together. "In Rome a thousand men are seeking you."

"It doesn't matter. We will go to Rome together. You will protect me. And from my hands you will receive ten times the sum which Sulla has promised you. Then you can go on your way."

The assassins put their heads together and decided to take Caesar back to Rome. The glitter of the gold he offered them was vivid in their minds. They waited until dark and then led him safely back to the city and through its streets to his mother's home. Here he found Cornelia and his baby Julia. And here it was that he paid the two assassins for sparing his life.

Caesar had been spared by the assassins but he was still not safe from Sulla. And while he hid in his mother's house his relatives and friends begged Sulla to forgive him. Through the efforts of his mother's brother, a distinguished aristocrat, and the Sacred College, Sulla was finally prevailed upon to pardon him. He gave in reluctantly. He had certain forebodings. "Take him," he said, "since you must have it so—but I predict that this youth for whom you plead so earnestly will one day overthrow the aristocracy. In this young Caesar goes another Marius."

Caesar was now free but he did not feel safe. And to escape the ruthless Sulla he left at once for Asia Minor where he joined a Roman army that was concluding the conquests of lands bordering on the Black Sea. He felt that if he were far from Sulla's sight he would be safe from his grasp. He planned to stay in Asia Minor until Sulla should die. "After all," he said, "Sulla has led a hard life as a soldier and he is now fifty-six years old. He is attending too many banquets and drinking too much wine. The luxuries of Rome are sure to drag him down. It will not take too long!"

Caesar became aide-de-camp to the commanding general and, although from the very first he felt a dislike for his new life, he nevertheless was interested in everything about him. He learned the details of military life and the responsibility of high officers. He also watched with keen interest how Roman provincial governments were set up and how the people reacted to their conquerors. And in one battle he distinguished himself by saving the life of a fellow soldier, for which he was awarded the "Civic Crown" of oak leaves.

After Caesar had been with the army in Asia Minor for a little more than two years, the long-awaited news of Sulla's death finally arrived and the young man quickly started back toward Rome. Since he did not like army life he had decided to enter politics and was anxious to set out in this new career at once.

However, he did not remain long at home. While he had been away his boyhood friend Marcus Cicero had won great fame for his oratory, and now that Caesar had definitely decided to enter politics he felt he would benefit by studying oratory with Cicero's old teacher Molo, on the island of Rhodes. It was to gain this end that he once more left Rome and started back toward the east. It was in the spring of the year 76 B.C.

But Caesar's trip was suddenly interrupted. Sailing in the Aegean Sea off the coast of Asia Minor, his ship was overtaken and captured by pirates. And he and the party of friends and servants with whom he was traveling were taken prisoners and brought to a near-by island where the pirates made their home. Here it was that the pirates planned to hold Caesar until his family paid a large ransom for his release. They demanded fifty thousand dollars and they sent several of his friends and servants back to get this sum.

At this time Caesar was twenty-four years old. He was fairly tall for a Roman and of a slight but muscular build. He had a keen and intelligent face, with a high, wide forehead, full lips and dark gray eyes. His complexion was pale and his nose was large and thin. He had a very even temper and pleasant personality and if he was angry at having been captured he did not show it. His manner was, as usual, calm and polite. He took the whole affair with ease. In fact, he laughingly chided the pirates for asking such a small ransom; he said that he was surely worth more!

The pirates liked Caesar. He had a magnetic personality and even these rough men were immediately attracted to him. During the six weeks that passed before his servants and friends returned with the money he spent long hours talking, argueing and laughing with them. Dressed in his toga, the mark of the Roman citizen, and with a golden belt hanging loosely around his waist, he joined freely in the life of his pirate captors. He never showed the slightest fear of them. He acted as though they were his bodyguard, not his captors. He boldly told them that once he was free he would come back and crucify them all. But the pirates only laughed. He joined in their sports and sang their songs. He recited poetry to them and delivered practice orations. And one day, when they were slow in applauding, he called them "illiterate barbarians" and said that for this alone they should all be crucified.

The pirates thought this a good joke. "Before you can crucify us," they said laughing, "you must first capture us. And with those clumsy Roman seamen of yours. . . ."

Then the arrogant pirate chief, unable to restrain himself, delivered a long lecture to Caesar on the superiority of pirates over Romans. He ended by saying, "Rome may be the center of the world, ruler of all lands, but she bows to us. The Mediterranean and Aegean are our seas. No ship passes without our permission. We hold the Senate in Rome in the palms of our hands. The only time when vessels sail the seas without fear is during the winter. And this is only true because at this season of the year we prefer to live in warm climates rather than sail the stormy seas."

As Caesar listened to the pirate's words and mocking laughter, the anger in him rose but he hid it as best he could. He knew that what the pirate said was true. Rome, the proud city of his birth, was a slave to the robber pirates that swept the blue seas.

But Caesar did not blame the pirates for his country's fate. He knew only too well, as did everyone in Rome, where to place the blame. It rested with a group of corrupt senators; men whose greed allowed them to put gold before the safety of the state. These men shared in the plunder which the pirates collected from the ships they captured, many of which were Roman ships.

It was because of these corrupt men and with their help that the pirates had been able to form a great armada of a thousand ships which swept the seas from the coast of Asia Minor to Gibraltar, from North Africa to Marseilles in southern Gaul. This fleet was divided into squadrons, each under an able commander. Every ship was armed. They stopped all vessels large or small. The pirates were so bold that they even landed on the shores of Italy, plundering towns and carrying off the inhabitants to be held for ransom or sold as slaves.

The island of Crete was completely in their power. The forests of Cilicia in Asia Minor supplied them with lumber for their vessels and the wild country, the bays and islands of this land, provided them with places where they could hide their captives and store their plunder.

All these things were well known to Caesar, but since he was not able, at this time, to correct them he brushed them aside. Besides, the problem of the pirates was only one of the pressing problems which confronted his country, and he knew that all were linked to the same corrupt senators. Someday, after he had entered politics, he might perhaps be in a position to do something about these things; at the moment he must be content with taking care of the situation which confronted him. And so he returned easily to joking and talking with the pirates.

In time Caesar's friends and servants returned with the ransom money. The pirates then took Caesar and his party to the mainland of Asia Minor and released them, saying that they could now continue without fear on their way to Rhodes. But Caesar did not go on his way. Instead he went to the near-by city of Miletus and collected a few armed vessels. With these under his command he returned at once to the pirates' island home. He knew exactly where to find it. And he surprised and captured them all. They were put in chains and carried back to the city of Miletus, where they were tried by the proper Roman officials. They were found guilty and condemned to death by crucifixion.

Caesar had warned the pirates that this was the manner of death they should expect. But now when the sentence was passed and he looked upon the miserable wretches and heard them begging for mercy, he interceded in their behalf. Crucifixion was a brutally cruel and lingering death and Caesar, who was a gentle person, could not bear the thought of it even for pirates. He asked that they first be killed and then nailed to the crosses. It was in this way that Caesar's captors met their death.

After all these things had taken place Caesar and his party sailed for Rhodes. Here, at last, he joined Molo, the great teacher of rhetoric and oratory. He worked hard and learned easily. And while he did not possess that very special gift which Cicero had for the spoken language, he nevertheless received from Molo a foundation in oratory which served him throughout his entire life. In time, he became known as second only to Cicero himself.

Caesar thoroughly enjoyed studying under the great teacher at Rhodes, but after he had been there only two years, his work was interrupted and he was forced to cut short his studies. News reached him that revolts had broken out in those countries bordering on the Black Sea where he had served in the Roman army. Since

Sulla's death, Rome had maintained very small forces in these lands and because of this the people had been encouraged to seek their freedom. And there were no proper military officers to lead the meager Roman forces. So although Caesar disliked military life and lacked authority from Rome, he felt that he must at once do something about the situation. The Roman Empire, he felt, must be placed before all other considerations.

And so it was that Caesar left Molo and Rhodes and went to the mainland of Asia Minor only a short distance away, where he collected a force of volunteers and Roman troops. Then quickly he set out for the troubled areas. He arrived in time to stem the spread of the disturbances and to secure the loyalty of some of the doubtful districts. Once having gained this position he held it until forces could arrive from Italy.

In time the reinforcements landed and Caesar was able to turn over his command to the regular army. He then started back home to Rome. Sailing across the Aegean he landed at Brindisi and then journeyed overland northward toward Rome.

Everywhere he went he was shocked by what he saw. What his father had told him years before when he was a little boy, he now saw with his own eyes. The farm lands were all held by rich absentee landlords and tilled by slaves; thousands upon thousands of slaves who were mercilessly worked until they fell in death and were then replaced by others from the bottomless reservoir of the provinces overseas. These slaves greatly outnumbered the native population and Caesar feared that they might one day rise up, throw off their chains and avenge themselves by murdering every Roman and citizen of Italy.

There were no small farms owned and cultivated by sturdy peasants. And every town and village was filled with idle mobs of homeless people, just like Rome. And Caesar knew whom to blame. The shocking condition of Italy rested squarely on the shoulders of those same senators, and their relatives and friends—about five hundred aristocratic families—who protected the pirates and who had supported the tyrant Sulla in his war against the people.

Caesar looked upon these men as a pack of wolves; men who because of their greed and complete disregard of life and liberty were bringing Rome and her growing Empire to the very brink of ruin. And as he traveled on he thought about the problem and of a possible solution.

He recalled that as a boy his tutor Gnipho had taught him that some years before two brothers by the name of Gracchi had recognized the seriousness of the situation and had fought for reforms. They demanded a redistribution of the land and an extension of the franchise. But they had been killed by their enemies in the senate class, and their bodies thrown like those of common criminals into the Tiber. The senators so hated these two brothers that they had actually forbidden their mother, who was the daughter of the great general Scipio, to wear mourning! Later Marius, his own uncle, had fought for these same ideals. He had succeeded in part. And the people of the Italian provinces had received the vote. But then Sulla had come along and wiped out the Roman Republic. And although it was true that since the tyrant's death the Republic had been more or less restored, the Senate was fighting very hard to retain as much power as possible.

These were some of the things Caesar thought about as he traveled on toward Rome. And he came to the conclusion that Rome must fall unless a leader could be found who would be strong enough, and wise enough, to fight the corrupt senators, strip them of the power they had usurped and bring Rome back to the democratic ideals of the old Republic.

Yes, a leader must be found, one who would be stronger and wiser than either the Gracchi or his uncle Marius.

And even though it did not occur to Caesar that he was the very person who had the ability and qualifications for the task, he decided at this time to devote his life to his country. He decided to do everything he could to bring about the needed reforms. He decided that he would work toward someday being elected consul, for as consul he would have the power to do what was needed. And even though he knew that before he could achieve this high post he would have to spend many years in other minor government positions, he was willing to do this in order to reach his goal.

Although Caesar was still a very young man he had the intelligence and vision to understand what was needed, the courage and ambition to want to carry out his ideals. He did not, however, know that this was to be his Destiny.

chapter
three

As soon as Caesar reached Rome he began to prepare himself for his political career. His defiance of the tyrant Sulla, his adventure with the pirates and his leadership in saving the eastern provinces had won him the admiration of the people of Rome. Still he did not feel that he was ready to run for election for even a minor office. He was aiming for the highest office in the land and so he did not want to rush in unprepared. He knew that success in politics required friends, influential friends. And so for the next three years he lived quietly at home with his mother, wife and little daughter, cultivating those who could be of help to him.

It was during this time that, as Caesar had feared, a great slave revolt shook Italy. A young slave named Spartacus, together with two hundred of his companions, broke out of a "stable" for gladiators in Capua, a city about one hundred miles south of Rome. These poor men were being trained to fight each other unto death as well as to defend themselves against wild beasts—skills they were later to display in the arenas in Rome for the pleasure and entertainment of the people!

The time was ripe, and as soon as it was known that two hundred men had revolted, three thousand other slaves from the surrounding country joined them. They made their headquarters in the crater of Vesuvius, which at that time was lying dormant. The news spread. In no time at all, slaves from every part of Italy joined the revolt and the life of every Roman and Italian was in imminent danger.

Roman soldiers were quickly sent into action. But the slaves were desperate and fought so bravely that it took the Roman legions two whole years to restore order. Spartacus and his men, using the crudest homemade tools and weapons, overran the entire peninsula, laying waste the farms of their old masters, defeating one Roman legion after another and capturing their eagles. In the end, however, the slaves were overwhelmed by the sheer numbers of Roman soldiers sent against them.

In a last bloody battle Spartacus and a great force of his men were surrounded and cut to pieces. Six thousand survived and were taken captive. And all these were later crucified. Their crosses lined the main highway for the entire one hundred miles from Rome to Capua. Their rotting bodies hung exposed for months so that all Romans might take comfort and all slaves take warning!

The two generals who finally succeeded in subduing the revolt were named Pompey and Crassus. Although Pompey was an extremely honest and forthright person, he had at one time served the tyrant Sulla. He had actually helped lead Sulla's troops in the march against Rome and the slaughter of the government forces. However, since that time he had won the people's admiration through a famous campaign in North Africa and had been honored with a Triumph, great parade and celebration, and also the title of "The Great."

Crassus had also served Sulla, but in a very different way. He had lent the tyrant money. Crassus was a rich man, the richest in all Rome, and there were many times when he was able to help Sulla. In return for this favor Sulla allowed Crassus to buy confiscated properties at bargain prices and he sold him the state mines. Crassus was also allowed the privilege of running a private fire department in Rome. His fire fighters went to all fires and sold their services on the spot. In this way Crassus was often able to buy burning buildings for very little; not until they belonged to him would he order his men to put out the flames. And so it was that in a few years the rich Crassus grew richer. His million-dollar fortune increased to two millions and then to twenty-five millions. This sum was as much as the whole yearly revenue collected by the Treasury of Rome, but Crassus saw no reason why he should not be as wealthy as the state itself. In fact he once said that he did not consider a man truly rich who could not raise, equip and maintain his own private army!

These were the two heros of the slave revolt, the generals who had saved Rome and Italy, and regardless of Crassus' questionable wealth, the citizens were so grateful that they elected them both to the office of consul in 70 B.C. This high office was usually reserved for those

who had served Rome in other political posts, but on
this occasion precedent was brushed aside and Crassus
and Pompey were thus rewarded. And Caesar, shrewdly
planning his political future, immediately became their
friends.

Caesar knew Pompey was an honest man, and he felt
that his popularity would be lasting. On the other hand,
Crassus had great influence among the rich business-
men of Rome and his money might at times be useful.
With two such friends, Caesar felt that he could not
fail. And so he now ran for his first public office. He was
content to start at the bottom of the political ladder. He
ran for "quaestor" and was elected. The year was 68
B.C. and Caesar was at this time thirty-two years old.

The two main governing bodies of the Roman Republic were a Senate and an Assembly. Senators held office
for life and were chosen from the aristocratic or senatorial class. During Caesar's time they numbered about
three hundred.

By custom senators brought their sons with them
when they were called into session. They wanted their
sons to learn the art of statesmanship, because many of
these boys would, of course, be senators themselves.
Some aristocratic Roman families served in the Senate
for several hundred years.

The Senate was the guardian of religion, controlled
the Treasury, appointed ambassadors and governors for
the provinces and decreed all public Thanksgivings and
Triumphs for victorious generals. It also served as a
court of justice for crimes such as treason and assassination, and it not only interpreted the laws but held
the power of repealing them if it chose.

The ordinary citizens gathered together, on the other hand, formed the Assembly, the highest authority in the state. And they exercised their power directly, not through representatives. This body was also a Court of Appeals. And the Senate and all public officials were sworn to obey the laws it passed and the decisions it reached.

Besides the senators and the Assembly, the Roman state had many officers which helped to run the government. Two consuls, the highest officers in the land, led the state in all the most sacred religious rites, presided over the Senate and the Assembly, suggested and executed laws and administered justice. During wartime they raised armies and funds for their support. If one consul died or was captured then the other ruled. If both died then a new election was ordered by the Senate.

In times of national peril the Senate had the power to declare an emergency and appoint either consul as "dictator" with complete power over everything except the Treasury. His term of office was limited to one year. This was the law but there were times, such as in Sulla's case, when the law was overlooked.

Beneath the two consuls there were ten tribunes, or representatives of the people's Assembly. Their main function was to act as a check on the Senate and to protect the people from bad laws or corrupt government. They could stop a law by just a single word "veto," which means "I forbid." Any citizen of Rome who was in distress could go to the home of one of these ten tribunes at any time of the day or night and demand a fair trial or ask for asylum.

There were also four praetors who led the armies in

war and whose job it was during peacetime to prevent and investigate crime; two quaestors who handled the state funds and acted as investigators of crime and corruption. They served as state prosecutors and were sometimes sent to a province as aid to the governor. Four aediles had charge of the streets, markets, public buildings, theaters, police courts and public games. And two powerful censors took care of a wide variety of state affairs. They chose the members of the Senate, which in Caesar's time numbered about three hundred, and took the census and examined the character of all candidates and public officials. They also watched over women, the education of children, treatment of slaves, collection of taxes, construction of public buildings and the letting of government contracts and the proper cultivation of the land. They also prepared and published the state budget.

All these officials, except the censors, were elected for a term of one year. The same office could be held by the same person only once every ten years and one year had to elapse before a man could run for a second office. And all candidates were expected to have served a certain length of time in the army before running for office.

This roughly was the set up of the Roman Republican government as it had evolved through the centuries since the overthrow of the Seven Kings. In theory it was democratic beyond all governments known in history. In practice, however, it was not so democratic. The aristocratic class whose members made up the Senate wielded entirely too much influence. Through their wealth and corruption they bought elections, judges and other officials. Thus by bribery they held enormous power. And in the years to come, Caesar's whole life was spent in an attempt to correct these evils and establish the government firmly on the democratic ideals of the Republic.

It was as quaestor that Caesar opened his political career. He was pleased with his election and he was assigned to the province of Spain as special aid to the Governor. But before taking up his duties abroad he was anxious to leave his imprint upon Rome. In order to impress indelibly upon the minds of the people that he would serve the democratic cause and devote himself to restoring the rights of the Assembly and the people's Tribune which Sulla had erased, he took a bold step. His aunt Julia, the widow of the great Marius, having just died, he used her funeral to recall to the people's minds the glories of Marius and the cause for which he had fought.

Since Sulla's reign the name of Marius had been unsafe to mention. But Caesar never knew the meaning of fear. He boldly ordered a bust of Marius and all his war trophies to be carried through the streets in the funeral procession. And when he delivered the funeral oration he not only reminded the crowds of his own distinguished birth by saying that Julia was directly descended from the gods, but he also spoke at length of Marius' glorious services to his country. And his words were so moving that veterans who had fought under his uncle came forward and with tears in their eyes saluted the trophies of their victories.

This funeral was followed by another. Cornelia,

Caesar's wife and the mother of his young daughter, died after a brief illness. She, too, was given a public funeral at which Caesar again delivered a moving oration. He reminded the crowds that his beloved Cornelia was the daughter of their last great democratic leader —Cinna.

Thus Caesar implanted in the minds of the people the hope that their rights would someday be restored; the hope that a new leader was coming to the fore. And in order to firmly cement his relations with Pompey and Crassus he now married Pompey's cousin Pompeia.

Having attended to all these things, Caesar now took up his duties in Spain. During the year of his term of office he went on a special judicial circuit and discharged his duties with intelligence and tact. But he suddenly seemed to become discouraged. He began to feel that he had started on his career too late in life. Visiting a temple of Hercules in some Spanish city, and coming upon a statue of Alexander the Great, he gazed upon it in silence for a long time. Then he spoke. "Here I am thirty-two years old. At this age, you, Alexander, had already conquered Egypt, Persia and India. Half the world lay at your feet. And I? What have I accomplished? Hardly anything." Then turning quickly he left the temple.

When his term of office in Spain was over, Caesar returned to Rome. But he did not go by boat across the Mediterranean as he had come, instead he traveled home by land. He was curious to visit Gaul and Cisalpine Gaul, the home of his old teacher Gnipho. And so he crossed the Pyrenees and traveled along the Mediterranean shore of southern Gaul.

The Gauls were tall, well built, muscular and strong. They had thick blond hair which they wore down to the nape of their necks, and many of the men had great flowing mustaches. They dressed in tunics made of bright-colored wools and embroidered with gay designs of flowers. And unlike the Romans they wore breeches. From their shoulders hung long striped cloaks. And they decorated themselves with as much jewelry and as many gold ornaments as they could afford.

They lived in walled towns and villages, built roads and bridged rivers. They farmed the land and had rich orchards and vineyards. They raised cattle and hunted, for they liked to eat great quantities of meat which they washed down with lots of beer and strong wine.

Caesar found the Gauls friendly. He spoke easily with them because he knew their language. Then crossing the Alps into Cisalpine Gaul he made his way down into Northern Italy, where the people held citizenship and enjoyed the right of voting.

Back home again in Rome, Caesar once more rejoined his friends Crassus and Pompey. But they were not to be together for long, because Pompey was now called upon to rid the Aegean and Mediterranean seas of pirates. The power of these outlaws had grown to such heights that even those corrupt men who were sharing in their loot felt that the time had come to call a halt. The pirates held such complete domination of the seas that Rome, which depended on Sicily, Sardinia and North Africa for her grain, was actually suffering from a serious shortage of food. And her foreign trade had been completely destroyed.

Pompey was the only Roman who could be entrusted

with this mission; everyone knew that he was completely honest and that he could not be bribed by the pirates. And so he was given command of a fleet and allowed three years to carry out this work.

But it did not take Pompey three years. In three brief months he had cleared the seas of every pirate. The last battle was fought in Cicilia, the pirate homeland. Thirteen hundred pirate ships were burnt. And everywhere their docks and arsenals were destroyed and their fortresses razed. And twenty-two thousand pirates were captured.

The swift annihilation of the pirates brought glory to Pompey and new disgrace to the Senate. It showed clearly that these outlaws had existed, not through real strength, but through the support of the senatorial class. And so when Pompey returned to Rome he was hailed as the people's hero and asked if he would serve them once more. Would he go to Asia Minor, the richest lands belonging to Rome, and subdue the spirit of revolt which still persisted?

Pompey undertook the task. And during the next few years he swept through Asia Minor conquering as he went. He carried the Roman eagles straight through to the river Euphrates. Then leaving a Roman fleet in command of the Black Sea, he continued on his victorious way. He marched his legions into Syria and took Antiochea. Tyre and Damascus surrendered next. Jerusalem was taken by storm. And with its fall Galilee, Samaria, Perea and Judea were added to the Roman Empire. Egypt and the island of Cyprus were the only lands which retained their independence.

In three short years, from 66 to 63 B.C., Pompey had

extended the Roman Empire over vast territories. He had conquered fifteen hundred cities and brought twelve million new people under Roman rule. He had established sound and lasting provincial governments, and the gold and silver which now flowed steadily into Rome filled the treasury to overflowing. And he returned to Rome the same way he had left, a poor man. He had not succumbed to the curse which tainted most Romans, the greed for gold.

chapter four

In 65 B.C. while Pompey was still in the East, Caesar took one more step up the political ladder toward the coveted post of consul. In that year he was elected as one of the four aediles of Rome.

Now the four aediles always divided between themselves the tasks which went with their office. And Caesar, wishing to establish a closer contact with the people, chose the management of the games in the arena as his work. The three other aediles took on the responsibilities of looking after the aqueducts, streets, markets and buildings.

Caesar did not personally enjoy the brutal displays of the arena, but in order to popularize his name with the common people he plunged into his new task with complete enthusiasm.

He rebuilt the stadium which was called the Circus Maximus, so that chariot races and other spectacles would have more room for action. The oval was ex-

larged so that its sides were almost half a mile long
and its width over two hundred yards across. Seats for
one hundred eighty thousand spectators were arranged
on three sides and beneath the stands stalls were built
where various foods and drinks were sold. Here, too,
were the stables for the racing horses, cages for the
wild beasts and barred pens for the slave gladiators.
When the work was completed the Circus Maximus
was more than twice as large as any stadium in America today.

In this stadium Caesar put on a variety of spectacles,
the grandeur of which had never been seen before. Besides foot races, wrestling, boxing and discus throwing,
Caesar entertained the people of Rome with what they
like best: chariot races—and gladiators in deadly combat with each other and with wild beasts.

These sports were so popular with the people that the
names of many charioteers and gladiators were known
to them and great sums of money were bet on favorites.
As the day for one of these contests approached, the
excitement in the city rose to a high pitch. And sometimes a poor gladiator, who was able to win the approval
of the audience by a particularly brave display in the
arena, was freed from slavery on the spot by the wild
acclaim of the mob. If a man survived three years as
a gladiator he automatically won his freedom, but very
few ever did.

Although Caesar was rather revolted by the spectacles of the arena, still he made it his duty to be present
at all times. It was he who officially opened each day of
contests and he was always there to receive the thank-

ful cheers of the mob. He was using these public displays for political gain.

After all the seats of the stadium were filled, Caesar would step into his private box. Having received the applause of the audience he would look about to see that the senators, generals and other distinguished citizens attending the games were settled in their boxes. Then he would give the signal for a trumpet to sound. With these piercing notes the chariots would come out from beneath the stands and slowly ride around the arena to the wild cheers of the crowd.

Depending on the race, the chariots were drawn by two, three or sometimes even four horses abreast. The drivers wore colorful tunics, highly polished metal helmets, and in their hands they held long whips and the horses' traces, which were also tied to their waist. And in their belts each carried a sharp knife with which he could free himself from the traces in case of accident. Naturally, wild upsets and accidents could always be expected.

After the sounding of the trumpet and when the charioteers had completed their slow ride around the arena to display themselves before the crowds, they took their places at the starting line. Then at a given signal the horses plunged forward. The race was on. The tension mounted quickly and the crowd went wild. Often men, horses and chariots piled up in mangled masses. And those who were able to race on were forced to steer clear of this wreckage. All this added to the excitement.

The usual chariot race consisted of seven laps around

the arena or about five miles. This was a terrific distance and extremely hard on both the horses and drivers. The center of the arena contained a narrow island about one thousand feet long which was adorned with columns and statues of the heroes of Rome. At each end of this island were heavy stone pillars which served as goals, and at one end there hung golden balls. As the race proceeded these were dropped one by one to mark the number of laps which had been covered. When the last ball was dropped the charioteers knew that they were racing for the finish line. And if the race was close when the last golden ball was dropped, the shouting, yells and wild outcries could be heard beyond the city limits.

Although chariot races were exciting, what the Romans liked best was to see bloody struggles of life and death. And Caesar did what he could to satisfy this public wish. He sometimes set two lines of gladiators, each consisting of one hundred or more men, against each other to imitate a real battle. At other times he had troops of archers try to defend themselves against hungry lions that were driven into the arena by attendants armed with whips, spears and red-hot irons. One day he had Negro slaves which he had brought from Africa fight some crocodiles from the Nile. Neither the Negroes nor the crocodiles seemed to care for the sport but they were both prodded on with spears and hot irons. Finally, to the great delight of the crowds, both men and animals were lying about in pools of blood, dead or dying.

But the greatest show that Caesar produced during his term as aedile was one in which a whole herd of elephants and a troop of trained gladiators fought each other. The elephants numbered one hundred and they were driven forward to meet the gladiators armed with javelins. The battle was indeed a fierce one. After the first few beasts were wounded the herd went wild. The men fought desperately to save themselves, but the elephants caught them in their trunks and hurled them high through the air. When the poor men crashed to the ground the maddened beasts then trampled them to death. In the end the entire arena was strewn with trampled bodies and massive dead or dying elephants. Many of these beasts, in their last agony, were on their knees with their trunks raised high, bellowing out pitifully. The mob in the stadium had never seen anything like this before and their cheers filled the air. On this day Caesar had given them thrills such as they had never known. He had given them a true Roman holiday. His name was on every lip. This was what he wanted.

Caesar knew the people of Rome. He understood their love for the dramatic and he used it to win their hearts. He spared no effort, no expense. And he succeeded in his scheme. When his term of office as aedile came to an end he had become—with the exception of Pompey who was still in the East—the most popular person in all Rome. Everyone knew his name. And the popularity which he gained through this means he never lost.

However, his success had cost him great sums of money. To reach his goal, he had spent more than the Senate allowed for public games. He had to pay the difference himself. It amounted to a quarter of a million dollars, and he was forced to borrow this sum from his friend Crassus. But Caesar did not worry. He was playing politics for high stakes. He was working to become consul and return Rome to democratic government. And he felt confident that he would someday be allotted a province to govern: this was the customary reward for public service. He would then quickly wipe out his debts and mend his own personal fortune.

With his term as aedile at an end and with the devotion of the people secured, Caesar now made his first real political move as the coming leader of the Popular party. He asked that an investigation be made into some of the doings of the dead tyrant Sulla. During Sulla's days many hundreds of completely innocent men had been murdered, their estates confiscated, their families ruined. Caesar asked that these cases be investigated and that justice be done. Public opinion was so strong that the Senate was forced to agree to his proposal. And he himself was appointed as chairman of the Committee of Investigation.

Naturally, this move by Caesar pleased the supporters of the old Popular party which had been virtually wiped out by Sulla. And in gratitude the people's Assembly elected Caesar as Pontifex Maximus. He moved at once into the official palace. Of all the honors to which a Roman citizen could aspire, that of Pontifex Maximus, or Pope of Rome, was the greatest. This office was held for life, was richly endowed and carried with it the dignity which is usually attached to religious positions. And although Caesar was not a religious person, he gladly accepted the honor. In fact he did everything in his power to be elected, running further into debt in order to defeat his two rivals, men of the senatorial class. However, Caesar need not have worked so hard, for his popularity was now so great that he won by a large majority. His votes were greater than those for the other two candidates combined.

With this great honor now his, Caesar prepared to run for praetor for the year of 62 B.C. And it was then that he met with his first real political opposition. The senatorial class had been watching his rise very closely and they now feared that Sulla's warning was coming true. His words—"This youth will someday overthrow the aristocracy. In this young Caesar goes another Marius."—now began to ring with a clear sound. They remembered the public display he had made of his uncle Marius' trophies at his aunt's funeral; they noted how proudly he always spoke of his first marriage to Cinna's daughter; they talked about the investigation he had conducted into Sulla's actions. And now he had defeated their two candidates for Pontifex! They felt that he was entirely too popular with the people and showed definite signs of following the path first indicated by the Gracchi; he must be stopped now before he progressed any further! And one of those who was loudest in voicing these fears was Cicero, his old childhood friend.

Cicero had also entered politics. He had started sooner and had preceded Caesar in all his elections. He was now a consul. And belonging to the Senatorial party he did everything in his power to cut off Caesar's career. Using his golden oratory, he spoke against him in the Senate and elsewhere. Even so, however, Caesar was elected praetor. And thus he rose one rung closer to the consulship.

It was during this same year that the victorious Pompey returned to Rome from the East. The senatorial

class, judging others by its own standards, was convinced
that he would bring his army with him and, like Sulla,
take Italy and Rome by force and become dictator.

But Pompey believed in law and order and such
thoughts were far from his mind. He landed at Brindisi
accompanied only by captive princes whom he hoped
would be paraded in his Triumph!

The aristocrats were stunned by his modesty. In fact
all of Rome was confused—all except Caesar. Now that
it was clear that Pompey would not seek political power,
Caesar pushed his own plans swiftly ahead. Thus the
month of December 62 B.C. marks the turning point in
his career.

Before this time, Caesar had played the game of politics as it was played in Rome at that time. He made
friends to gain influence and money. He used money to
gain popularity. He used his popularity to gain power.
But once within easy reach of his goal, a change took
place in his methods.

Caesar now felt strong enough, secure enough, to
stand on his own character. He was an extremely intelligent person, honest and compassionate, and from now
on he allowed his true nature to rule. Whatever unethical
methods he had indulged in, he had used only as a means
toward an end, an end which he felt was greater than
anything else. He dreamed of taking the government
out of the hands of the corrupt senatorial class and of
establishing a truly democratic rule, one which would
not only serve Rome but also its great Empire. He felt
that this was essential if the Roman Empire were to
survive. And from this time on he dedicated his life to
the welfare of his country.

chapter five

WHEN CAESAR'S YEAR as praetor had expired he was appointed by the Senate as military governor of Spain. This was a welcome appointment for now he would be able to repay Crassus the huge sum of money which he owed him and also mend his own personal fortune. All Roman governors amassed great wealth in their provinces. This was an accepted custom. And Caesar was no different from the others. But besides mending his own fortune he managed to collect huge sums of money which he sent home to Rome. Such gifts to the Treasury were always welcomed.

However, Caesar, unlike most governors, did not neglect his official duties. With his usual directness and interest he at once began the task of completing the conquest of the peninsula, a conquest which had begun in the days of Scipio and Hannibal. He quickly quenched the embers of rebellion that were still smoldering. And he waged two minor campaigns against some wild hill tribes who had been raiding the villages and settlements in the prosperous valleys. Then he turned his attention to ruling. He revised laws, settled quarrels, abolished certain barbaric customs and conferred honors and privileges upon those who were worthy.

What Caesar accomplished he accomplished quickly, but his work was done with complete thoroughness. He left no festering spots that would break out at some later date. And when his term of office ended he left behind him a well-organized, healthy province.

Leaving Spain, Caesar sailed directly for Rome. This time he did not take the long journey overland through Gaul, but returned by sea so that he could arrive in Rome in time for the elections. Now, he felt, he was ready to run for the highest office in the land. He was forty-one years old and he felt his apprenticeship was over. He had served in many positions. He had proven his ability. He was ready. He ran for consul.

The Senate had expected that Caesar would do this very thing and they fought him with every means at their command. But again he won without difficulty. The people loved him and wanted him. And furthermore he was backed by the wealthy Crassus and the triumphant Pompey—Pompey who had swept the seas clear of pirates and who had only recently returned in glory after conquering the whole of Asia Minor, Syria and the lands of the Hebrews.

But once Caesar had obtained the high office of consul he was faced by many opposing forces, confronted by many political enemies. Even Marcus Bibulus, his co-consul, worked against him. This man was a friend of the Senate. He was a dull, obstinate person whom the aristocrats knew they could count on to resist Caesar at every turn. Bibulus, they hoped, would be able to restrain Caesar during his term of office, and when Caesar's consulship should expire they plotted to appoint him head of a department which they called the "Woods and Forests." They would not appoint him governor of a province which was the customary reward for those who had served as consuls. They did not want him to command an army. In this way they hoped to bury him politically.

But things did not work out as the aristocrats had planned. Caesar understood his enemies and he was not afraid. Having spent many years preparing to become consul, now that he had achieved his goal he had no intention of being brushed aside. He was determined to bring about many needed reforms. He had dedicated his life to one cause—to work for the good of all the people and toward the survival of the Roman Empire. And the Senate soon learned that they were dealing with a masterful person, one whom they could not control.

Caesar's very first act was aimed against the corrupt Senate. It was a democratic law. It ordered that all the transactions of the Senate must be made public. A summary of the debates and proposed bills must be posted each day in the Forum for all to see. There were to be no more secret decisions, no more private manipulations. By this order the Senate at once became more representative and responsible to the people.

Caesar's second act was designed to help the veterans of the long wars and to find peaceful occupations for them. It was designed to rehabilitate the homeless population of Rome and strengthen the national fiber by building up a class of small farmers. Caesar proposed to give each of the thousands of veterans a piece of good land so that he and his family could farm it and thus enjoy a small measure of security. He proposed that the state should buy this land from the wealthy landowners, paying them a fair price. And the money? The money was to come from the Treasury, which was overflowing with the loot of military conquests. Thus the soldiers who conquered for Rome would receive a share of the spoils of war. This seemed only just. Yet the powerful aristocrats immediately came out in opposition to it. Day after day the members of the Senate argued bitterly against it. Some even said that soldiers did not know how to farm and that it would therefore be useless to give them land.

Since Caesar had expected the Senate to behave in just this way, he was fully prepared. He decided to return to the democratic method which had been followed in the old Republic before Sulla had stripped the people of their rights. He decided to present his bill directly to the people's Assembly. He knew that land reforms were essential for the survival of Rome.

The Senate rose in fury, but Caesar's will was firm. And it was in this way, by direct appeal to the people, that his land bill became law. This was Caesar's first bitter clash with the Senate and he won a decisive victory.

Casting aside all reason, the angry Senators now decided to vote against everything Caesar might propose. In their stupidity and greed they failed to understand that if they would give up a little of their vast holdings in order to make life bearable for the many, the state could survive; if they persisted in their blindness and greed the state would fall and they would fall with it. They looked upon Caesar as their enemy, failing to understand that he was as much their friend as he was a friend of the people.

Caesar was not stopped by his enemies, however. He clashed again and again with the Senate. But in these bitter battles he always won. Over the loud protests of the senators he took his proposed laws directly to the people. Thus it was that he obtained legislation against sacrilege, bribery at elections, the debasing of the coinage and also corrupt state contracts. He also passed a law which made it a serious offense for judges to accept bribes and another which required the governors of provinces to have their accounts inspected.

As Caesar's year of office was drawing to a close the Senate was much relieved. And many senators whispered to each other, "Now we can bury him. Now he shall become the director of "Woods and Forests." At last we shall be rid of him. And when he is out of the way we will repeal all his reforms and laws. We don't need them!"

But Caesar had other ideas. He had no intention of having his laws repealed. And so he did everything he could to assure the election of two members of the Popular party as the next consuls. And to cement his bond of friendship with Pompey he gave him his daughter Julia in marriage. As for himself he wanted to serve his country and he knew exactly where this could be done. The German hordes were again crossing into Gaul and Caesar knew that it would not be long before they would once more threaten the Italian provinces and Rome. If the Senate would give him legions, he volunteered to go into the little-known lands of Gaul and force the Germans back into their own territories. He would make Gaul into a buffer state between Italy and the lands of the barbarians.

The Senators who had dreamed of losing Caesar in the depths of the "Woods and Forests" were not too pleased with his idea. They did not want to give him legions to command. Yet they feared that if they refused, the people would act without them. Besides, "Gaul is vast and the natives are barbarians," they said. "Caesar will not have an easy time. He has had his own way too long; now let him taste the bitterness of defeat. With defeat the people will lose their love for him."

"Yes, let him go to Gaul," the senators agreed. "Life here in Rome will be better without him. Besides, he may never return. The lands to the north are vast and dangerous. He may die."

And so it was that with these whispers and sentiments the senators made Caesar governor of Cisalpine Gaul and Illyria. And they gave him unlimited freedom to do as he chose in the lands that we now know as France, Belgium, Switzerland, part of the Netherlands and the Rhineland of Germany! And they placed four legions under his command.

To these legions Caesar added four more which he equipped at his own expense. And during the following years he invaded Gaul and brought it into the Roman Empire.

This famed Roman army of Caesar's was made up of legions, each of which consisted of about four thousand infantry, three hundred cavalry and small companies of specialized troops trained as engineers or skilled in the use of certain weapons. Each legion was divided into centuries. A century originally consisted of one hundred men, but later it grew to two hundred. And over each of these divisions a centurion, or captain, was in command. Every legion had its own flag which the men defended with their lives.

Each first-class infantry man was armed with several javelins, a dagger and a short sword. Some also carried bows and arrows. For protection the soldiers wore bronze helmets, breastplates, greaves, which covered their legs from knee to ankle, and shields. Second-class soldiers had all this equipment except the breastplates, while the third and fourth classes had no armor at all. And the fifth class was only provided with slings and stones. The slingers and archers were attached to the light-armed companies, but had no special positions. Unhampered by heavy gear, they were swift and could quickly be assigned to any battle position.

While on the march, each soldier carried a heavy pack which contained food enough for fifteen days, mostly grain. The pack also contained cooking utensils, a saw, a basket, a mattock, an ax, a hook, a leather thong, a chain and a number of tent stakes. This load weighed sixty pounds. And with this pack on his back and carrying his weapons, the Roman soldier often marched twenty or more miles in a single day. And at the end of each day they built a camp completely surrounded by a protecting trench and enbankment of earth! They were powerful men and of great endurance.

The high Roman officers rode horseback. In this way they could travel quickly from one position to another whether on the march or on the field of battle. Caesar himself rode a very famous horse which he had bred in his own stables. This horse was fiery and swift and had never known another rider. It was said that no one had ever been able to mount him except Caesar.

The Roman army rarely used wagons, for they were considered too cumbersome. Beasts of burden carried the tents, mills for grinding the grain, baggage and supplies.

The Roman soldier ate twice a day. The meal in the middle of the day was light, and their main meal was in the evening after the long march or the end of fighting. They ate bread, cooked cereals, vegetables and meat. Oddly enough, they preferred vegetables—and sometimes when they were short of grain they complained about having too much meat to eat! They drank a light sour wine and added vinegar to their water, believing that bad water was thus rendered harmless.

The men of the Roman army were self-sufficient. In foreign lands they made everything they needed. They made and mended their own clothes, made sandles, ground grain for bread, repaired their weapons and armor and forged tools and new weapons as needed. They knew how to plow and reap, how to build camps, forts, bridges and ships that could ride a rough sea. In every possible craft and work necessary to their survival, the Roman soldiers displayed the greatest of skill.

On the field of battle the bravest and best-armed men made up the front lines. These fearless men were trained to move in close to the enemy. When they were only about ten or fifteen paces away they threw their javelins, and at this signal the archers and slingers then began their attack with arrows and stones. Then when the last javelins had been hurled, the soldiers drew their short swords and moved in for hand-to-hand combat. In this manner they fought the enemy.

The Roman army had several ways of attacking walled cities and forts. They had developed huge wooden catapults capable of hurling rocks over high walls, and battering rams for pounding and crumbling stone fortifications. These rams were constructed of heavy timers suspended from a frame by chains or ropes, and it sometimes took a hundred men to set one in motion. The Romans also attacked walled cities by building tall wooden towers from the top of which their archers could send arrows down upon the defenders.

The art of war was highly developed in ancient Rome. Roman boys were trained from infancy in the use of weapons. They were strictly disciplined and courage was demanded at all times. Each youth was required to spend ten years in the army.

Heroes were rewarded and cowardice could be punished by death. Generals had the right to cut off the heads of any who deserted during battle. The brutal spectacles of the circus games in Rome made men familiar with death. Their hearts were hardened and their training gave them a thirst for victory.

Such was the make-up of the Roman army and the character of its soldiers. These were the men who had conquered Italy, North Africa, Spain, Greece and the Near East. And these were the soldiers that Caesar was now leading into Gaul.

Caesar was forty-three years old at this time. And although he was remarkably healthy, for he had always lived a simple life, still it was rather late to start out on a military career. It was all the more so for a man who had never shown any interest in war and who had spent but two short periods with the army; once in Asia Minor and once in Spain. And now that he was going into the wild and unknown regions north of the Alps, his enemies hoped and believed he would never return.

But at this time no one in Rome, not even Caesar himself, knew what the future held. No one dreamed that in Gaul Caesar would begin a military career which we today value as equal to those of Alexander the Great, Genghis Khan and Napoleon.

chapter six

CAESAR'S FIRST CAMPAIGN in Gaul was directed against the Helvetii, a tribe of rugged mountain people who occupied that part of Gaul which we now know as Switzerland.

The Helvetii had for generations been exposed to the attacks of the barbaric Germans and had finally decided to leave their homeland and migrate to more peaceful and fertile lands westward. And so they burned their villages, piled their wagons with their goods and provisions and took off with their women, children, cattle, horses, pigs and dogs. They numbered three hundred thousand people and of these ninety thousand were fighting men.

Caesar understood the problem which confronted the Helvetii, but knowing that their vacated lands would immediately be occupied by the barbarian Germans and offer a threat to Italy and Rome, he determined to stop them. With a swiftness of action, which was many times in the future to strike terror into the hearts of his enemies, Caesar blocked their path. Leading one Roman legion and some troops of friendly Gauls, he hurried north to Geneva. Here, cutting the bridge which spanned the Rhone, he took his stand.

Then he spoke with the Helvetians and, assuming a friendly manner, told them that they could not migrate into Gaul proper without permission from Rome. He asked them to wait. He said that in two weeks they would receive a reply. The Helvetians believed Caesar and in this way he was able to gain time. He quickly threw up forts, dug trenches and raised walls at every point where the river might be crossed. When all was ready, he then announced that Rome had refused their request.

The Helvetii, however, were determined to continue on their way. They tried to cross the river in boats; they attempted to ford it. But although they greatly outnumbered the Romans they were completely unable to force their way through. And so they finally decided to change their route; they turned northwest.

Caesar, determined to force them back into their own territory, decided to block their way once more. To accomplish this he needed more troops. Therefore, leaving his legion under the command of a trusted general named Labienus, he hurried back alone to Cisalpine Gaul for reinforcements. And in seven days he returned at the head of five fresh legions!

When the Helvetii saw this well-equipped Roman army they begged for peace. They asked to be allowed to settle somewhere in Gaul, wherever Caesar should choose. But Caesar was determined to send them back to their own land. And when their request was refused they decided to fight.

In a single battle, which lasted from noon until night-fall, the Helvetii were completely defeated and their migration was stopped. Half the Helvetian fighting force was killed. They were brave men and they fought with great courage, but the battle was one between wild valor and Roman skill and discipline.

Caesar treated the conquered Helvetii with great kind-ness and wisdom. He asked for neither spoils nor cap-tives. He simply ordered them back into their own prov-ince. He even supplied them with food sufficient to last until the next harvest.

In this very first campaign, Caesar proved himself a brilliant military leader and a diplomatic victor. The Hel-vetii had been beaten but they carried back with them no bitterness nor passion for revenge. Caesar's generous terms of peace astonished and impressed all Gaul. And the people of Gaul thought that if they were friendly to Caesar he might help them hold back the German hordes that were always threatening their borders. So envoys came from every tribe to thank Caesar and to vow eternal friendship.

And those from the lands bordering the Rhine told him that one hundred twenty thousand Germans had already crossed the river and settled in Gaul; they had taken by force some of the best lands. These envoys also warned that more were coming.

"Their leader is a cruel chieftain named Ariovistus," they said. "It is he who has led the invasion. He boldly declared that his people wanted to exchange their for-ests for our rich cultivated fields. And when we refused he made war against us. He has set himself up as ruler of the entire district, demanding obedience from us as well as from his own people. He has even taken the children of some our leaders and is holding them as hostages. He tortures them cruelly to force us into submission."

Caesar listened carefully. Then after considering the situation he sent envoys to the German chief, asking him to name a time and place where they might discuss matters.

But Ariovistus was arrogant. He replied, "If I wanted anything of Caesar, I would go to him. If Caesar wants anything of me, he should come to me."

When these words were reported to Caesar, he immediately sent word to Ariovistus that all hostages must be returned at once to the Gauls and that no more Germans must cross the Rhine. If these terms were not complied with immediately, Caesar said that he would lead his legions forward.

But Ariovistus was defiant. He answered that he had never interfered with Rome and that Rome, therefore, had no right to interfere with him. He further said that he would keep the hostages and that since the Gauls whom he had defeated were now his vassals, he resented Caesar's interest in them. And to all this he added the following, "I may say that no one ever opposed me without bringing himself to ruin. For fourteen years my Germans have not known a roof over their heads. They are past masters in the science of war. Enter the battle when you choose, and learn the extent of their uncontrollable might."

But Caesar was not frightened by these boastful words. He at once began a series of forced marches northward to a place called Besançon. He then ordered his troops to build a fortified camp. From here he planned to seek out and attack Ariovistus and his army.

However, a strange thing suddenly occurred. The local Gauls, in their fear of the northern barbarians, told Caesar's men all sorts of weird tales about the Germans. They said that they were all giants of unbelievable strength and daring. And that the gaze of their cold blue eyes was so penetrating that it could not be borne.

As a result of this, many of Caesar's soldiers and officers took fright. Some made excuses and asked for leave, while others stayed in their tents, writing last letters to friends and relatives and making out their wills. The entire camp was gripped with fear and Caesar was told that the army would follow him no farther into this unknown land, a land where Romans had never been before.

But Caesar was determined, feeling that he could inspire his men and give them confidence. He called them together and addressed them.

"The Germans," he said, "are no different from other barbarians. Did not the Helvetii fight them off for years? And did not my own uncle, the great general Marius, defeat them when they threatened Rome? I ask you to believe in me. My life bears witness to my character. And our victory over the Helvetii should prove to you my ability as a general. Besides, Roman legions never mutiny!"

Caesar's words brought confidence and courage to his men, all swearing they would follow him wherever he might lead them. And on the following evening they set out in search of Ariovistus, making contact with his advance forces six days later.

Ariovistus was now less arrogant. He quickly sent envoys to Caesar proposing a meeting.

The two leaders, each accompanied by a small guard of cavalry, met on the top of a knoll situated in the center of a broad plain that separated their forces.

Caesar was the first to speak. He said that Rome only desired her allies and friends to grow and prosper; the Gauls must not be robbed of what they possessed. Then he asked Ariovistus to return the hostages he held and he sought a promise that no more Germans would cross the Rhine into Gaul. Those, he said, who had already settled might remain.

To this Ariovistus replied that he first wanted Caesar to understand that he was a great German king, that he had committed no act of aggresion; he had only crossed the Rhine because the Gauls had invited him. They had given him the land which his people now occupied and the hostages were really only his guests. Then suddenly growing very angry he shouted, "Unless you withdraw your forces you will meet death!"

After this outburst Ariovistus grew calmer and changed his tone. He told Caesar that certain senators in Rome had contacted him and promised him great honors if he should capture and kill Caesar. However, this did not seem to interest him. Instead, he wanted the honor of the battle and offered Caesar a great sum of money if he would withdraw his forces.

When Caesar refused, Ariovistus again grew angry and began to shout at him. Caesar then called off the negotiations and with his guard rode back to the Roman camp. War could not be avoided.

For the next five days Caesar paraded his forces in front of the enemy camp. But the Germans refused to fight. This was rather puzzling. But then Caesar learned that it was the custom among the Germans for certain women, priestesses, to decide by signs and magic the best time for battles; and they had declared that Fate would be against a German victory if they fought before the new moon!

At length Ariovistus moved his troops into battle position. And to make retreat impossible he surrounded his lines on three sides with his many transport wagons. These were filled with women and children, who, sensing danger, wept and implored their menfolk to make sure they did not fall captive to the Romans.

So furious was the first Roman onrush, so swift and sudden, that the soldiers did not have time to hurl their javelins. The two armies fought hand to hand. Then Caesar's cavalry thundered forward. It appeared suddenly as from nowhere and this surprise attack turned the tide of battle.

Terror seized the Germans. Abandoning their women and children, they ran for their lives. They headed toward the Rhine, fifteen miles away. But the Romans pursued and cut them down. Only a small number escaped. Some swam across the river; others found boats.

Ariovistus was among those who escaped. He abandoned his army and his two wives and children. Caesar had hoped to capture him. He pursued him right to the riverbank. But Ariovistus managed to escape into Germany. And he was never heard of again.

Caesar was disappointed. However, he was rewarded in another way. He came upon the children of the Gauls whom the Germans had held as hostages and he was happy to liberate them and return them to their families.

In this way did Caesar's first summer in Gaul come to an end. He was content with the two campaigns he had fought and with his victories. And leaving his legions under the command of Labienus, in winter quarters at Besançon, he returned to Cisalpine Gaul to attend to the administration of his province.

But during the winter, while he was away, he heard disturbing news about the Belgium tribes that inhabited what is today northern France, Belgium and a part of the Netherlands. These people, who numbered about one third of all the people of Gaul, were extremely hostile to the Romans and were in league with the Germans. They resented Roman troops wintering in Gaul and feared that the Romans would in time attack them and force them into bondage.

Caesar at once raised two more legions in Cisalpine Gaul and sent them across the Alps to join Labienus and his other forces. Then at the first sign of spring he followed. And suddenly, before the Belgiums knew what had happened, he and his entire army were on the river Marne.

He had again acted with decision and amazing speed. Once more he had taken his enemy by surprise, and the first Belgium tribe, the Remi (people of Rheims), surrendered without resistence. However, they told Caesar that the other Belgiums were determined to fight.

There were six main tribes, the Nervii being the fiercest of all, and their collective force numbered about three hundred thousand.

But Caesar did not hesitate. Sending a legion under the command of the son of his friend Crassus to conquer the Atlantic seacoast tribes, he and his other legions headed north. And as they marched on, one tribe after another surrendered without resistance.

Caesar, with his usual wisdom, treated them all with a kindness almost unknown at that time. He took only a few hostages to insure their future good behavior. But the strongest and fiercest tribe of the Belgians remained defiant. The Nervii were a proud people and they refused to bid for peace. Besides, they were expecting aid from the Germans and, therefore, felt confident that they could defeat the Roman enemy.

Caesar set out at once for their land, a place to which no Romans had ever gone before. It was in the territory which today surrounds the modern city of Brussels. He wanted to prevent the Nervii from joining forces with their German allies. He could then fight them separately. Caesar pushed his legions forward and sent scouts ahead to choose a good campsite somewhere on the Sambre River. But there were some Gauls who had been traveling with Caesar's army who suddenly deserted and went to warn the Nervii.

When the legions finally reached the chosen campsite the Roman soldiers at once set to work entrenching and fortifying the place. Completely innocent of the fact that a vast horde of sixty thousand enemy soldiers was hidden in the thick surrounding forest, they broke ranks and, laying aside their arms, took up their axes, spades and mattocks.

Suddenly the enemy attacked. The surprise was complete and the Romans were thrown into wild confusion. Some of the light-armed troops fled. But the legionnaires, with unbelievable courage, picked up their arms and singly or huddled together in small groups tried desperately to fight back. Even the wounded, leaning on their shields, fought on. For a time it looked as though all would be lost but the discipline, experience and intelligence of the individual Roman conquered over the wild tactics of the barbarians. In time a few legions managed to form battle lines and hold the enemy on the right.

Caesar, however, standing on the crest of a low hill and looking down upon the scene, knew that the greatest courage in the world could not, alone, change the tide of battle. All the ranks must be re-formed and the standards and colors must once more lead.

Rushing down into a group of standard-bearers huddled together in fear, he ordered them to the front. Then grabbing a shield and a sword from a soldier he ran bareheaded into the midst of the battle. His scarlet cape could be seen from many parts of the field. At once the men's spirits rose.

Caesar addressed the centurions by name and called upon the men to form ranks. He went from one end of the field to the other, urging them on. And the men, inspired by his presence and taking strength from the honor and tradition of the Roman army, managed to fight their way back to their battle positions. Then once more behind their honored standards and colors they faced the enemy.

The Nervii were soon checked. But they fought on, preferring death to defeat. As their ranks fell, they piled up the bodies of their dead and from the top of these mounds they hurled spears and rocks down upon the Romans. In the end only five hundred men remained out of the sixty thousand who had launched the attack.

In this way a near Roman rout was turned into a great victory. But Caesar and his men were still not finished with their task. After only a short rest they had to turn back toward the city of Namur to engage the German allies of the Nervii. These barbarian forces, coming too late for the battle, had barricaded themselves behind the wall of this strongly fortified city. They were very big men, almost a race of giants, and when they first laid eyes on the small Romans they were filled with contempt. But when they saw the Romans dragging forward great siege towers and battering rams they lost heart and quickly begged for peace.

Caesar promised to spare their lives and let them return to their homes if they would turn over all their arms. They agreed. They came to the top of the city wall and threw down their swords and lances until the moat was filled. Then they opened the gates of the city and formally surrendered.

The Romans, however, did not occupy Namur, for Caesar feared treachery. And he was right. The Germans had not surrendered all their arms; they had hidden one third. And in the middle of the night they stole out of the city and attacked the sleeping Romans. Fortunately, Caesar had provided for such an event. He had made his men prepare great piles of brush and wood in convenient places. These were at once set ablaze and by their bright light his legions fought the Germans.

After a desperate battle the barbarians were driven back into the city, leaving four thousand dead and wounded. And the following morning they surrendered without reservations.

Caesar decided to make an example of these treacherous Germans. Until now he had treated all vanquished people with the greatest generosity. He had always shown respect for those who fought bravely to defend their homeland, no matter how hard they had made it for him to conquer them. But treachery was unforgivable. He rounded up all the Germans within Namur and turned them over to the slave contractors, who always followed Roman armies. It has been recorded that on that day fifty three thousand were sold into slavery.

In this way did Caesar's second summer in Gaul come to a close. The Belgians were completely crushed and brought under Roman dominion. And the Germans beyond the Rhine now sent peace envoys to Caesar with offers of friendship.

chapter

seven

WHEN THE NEWS of Caesar's latest victories in Gaul reached Rome, the senators were forced to order an extraordinary Thanksgiving of fifteen days. They did not want to do this but they were powerless against the clamor and sentiment of the public. The people, who had always liked Caesar, now hailed him as their deliverer. He had proven himself a great reformer and had fought for them in the Senate. Now he had also proven himself a great military leader and had eliminated the threat of a barbarian invasion from the north. His name was spoken everywhere, in every town and hamlet in Italy, in every home and on every street in Rome.

But while Caesar's name was hailed by the people, it was spoken of in a different manner by his enemies in the Senate. Since Ariovistus had failed them, they now planned to prevent Caesar from winning any further glories and they discussed endless ways to accomplish this.

71

These men had still not learned the obvious lesson that if the Empire were to survive they must adjust to the changing times, accept the reform of certain social ills and set aside their greed for gold. They continued in their blind belief that they could use their legislative powers for their selfish ends, ignoring the needs of the people and the state. They continued to drain millions from the Roman provinces to add to their personal fortunes. They built palaces for themselves and wallowed in luxury while others starved. And they tried hard to repeal the reforms which Caesar had put through. However, since Pompey, Crassus and many of Caesar's friends fought them, they were not too successful.

Now with the news of Caesar's second victorious summer and the acclaim of the people, these same evil senators planned to end Caesar's career. If they were to survive, they reasoned, they must get rid of him. The great German chieftain Ariovistus had failed them. And Caesar had not perished from the rigors of a soldier's life as they had hoped. There was only one way now left open to them. They would act boldly; they would recall him on some pretext or other and would repeal all his laws. And so a motion was at once introduced in the Senate to revise Caesar's Land Act.

Now Pompey was committed to support this law, for Caesar had instituted it, in part, to provide for his soldiers who had fought so bravely and then had been disbanded without any consideration. He felt that he was honor bound to give Caesar his complete support on this matter. And so he sent a special messenger north to warn Caesar of what his enemies were planning. The result was that a conference of Caesar's friends and the leaders of the Popular party was immediately called to discuss the crisis. This meeting was held at Lucca, a town on the boundary of Caesar's province. Among those who attended were Pompey, Crassus and a hundred friendly senators.

With Caesar, Pompey and Crassus once more united, a definite plan for fighting the corrupt senators and regaining control of the government was decided upon. Pompey and Crassus were to run for consuls for the coming year. When their terms had expired Pompey was to go to Spain as governor and Crassus to Syria. Caesar's command in Gaul was to be extended for five years after his present term expired; he did not want to leave Gaul half conquered. Besides, he was hoping to run for consul a second time. And since it was the law that ten years must elapse between two consulships, this extra term in Gaul would fulfill the requirements.

The senators who were present promised their support for these plans. And since the elections were to be held during the winter, when Caesar's soldiers were on furlough in Rome, the popular vote was assured.

But when Pompey, Crassus and the friendly senators returned to Rome their enemies united against them. They refused to accept the names of Pompey and Crassus for the consulships and they tried to prevent the elections from taking place. They made endless speeches in the Senate. They ranted on, hour after hour. Some had to be bodily removed for exceeding the time allowed for speeches. They fomented riots. They even said that the stars in the heavens were not auspicious, and that everything must be postponed. But all in vain. The people would not listen. They wanted to vote. And Pompey and

Crassus were elected, while Caesar's term in Gaul was extended for another five years.

Now during these same winter months, which ended with the conference at Lucca, Caesar received news of a coming revolt in Brittany. The Veneti, the most important of the coastal tribes, were planning to free themselves from Roman domination.

The people were sailors and fishermen and were very ingenious, industrious and independent. They had a large fleet of sturdy ships which could sail the heavy seas along their coast. Their flat-bottomed boats had high bows and sterns and were built of oak with heavy timbers a foot thick, fastened with great iron nails. They had iron chains and sails made of leather. In these vessels the Veneti traded up and down the Bay of Biscay and along the British Channel. Although they were unwieldly, the Veneti managed them with ease. They even sailed to distant Britain.

The settlements of the Veneti were on the many rocky islands and promontories along the Atlantic coast between Brest and the river Loire. At high tide they were completely cut off from the mainland and could be reached only by water. Because of this these people felt that they could easily fight off Roman attacks; the Romans might be masters on land but they could not also be masters of the sea. And so they revolted and killed several Roman officers who were sent among them on official business.

Caesar knew that if the Veneti were not punished, their spirit of defiance would spread to neighboring tribes and a large-scale revolt would develop. He therefore determined to prove to all Gaul that Rome would tolerate neither treachery nor impatience with her rule.

He ordered a fleet of galleys to be built at once along the banks of the Loire. And he sent a force of special oarsmen, seamen and pilots from Marseilles to man these galleys. Then with the coming of spring and after the conference at Lucca, he left Cisalpine Gaul and joined his forces.

A great sea battle followed. It was fought off the promontory of Quiberon and lasted from ten in the morning until sunset. The Roman fleet was under the command of an able young officer named Decimus Brutus. And Caesar and his army stood on the shore and watched.

The swift Roman galleys engaged two hundred and twenty of the cumbersome ships of the Veneti. But speed was the only advantage which the Romans had. The Veneti were excellent sailors and knew every movement of their waters. Besides, their ships were too heavily built to be run down and they rose so high above the galleys that it was not possible for the Romans to attack them with javelins.

Hour after hour the battle continued, neither side being able to gain an advantage. Then suddenly the tide of battle changed. The ingenious Romans brought out sickles attached to long poles and, sweeping swiftly alongside of the enemy ships, they cut the ropes which held the leather sails. The sails fell and the ships were helpless. Then the galleys closed in and the Romans boarded the vessels, killing and capturing all on board.

This sea battle marked the end of the Veneti revolt. With their fleet completely destroyed, these Gauls could no longer resist. They surrendered. And to warn all

Gauls against following the example of the Veneti, Caesar dealt very brutally with these brave people. He killed their leaders and sold the entire tribe — men, women and children—into slavery.

Now while Caesar was occupied in Brittany a few of his legions, under young Crassus, fought a campaign against some tribes to the south close to the Pyrenees. These people had allied themselves with neighboring Spaniards and were determined to resist Roman domination. However, they were swiftly subdued. And so it was that by the end of the third summer, Caesar had completely conquered Gaul. Through unusual military and diplomatic ability he had, with an amazingly small loss of men, accomplished what no one else had ever done before.

Gaul was still not to know peace. During the winter months which followed, another dangerous immigration of barbarian Germans took place. Heedless of the fate of Ariovistus, several smaller tribes crossed the Rhine and began to settle on the lands of the Belgians.

In the spring Caesar led his troops against them. The Germans begged to be allowed to remain where they were, for they said they could not return to their former homes. They insisted that they had been driven across the Rhine against their will. A powerful nation of savages from the northern wastelands had pushed them out of their own territory. These people, they said, were nomads who lived by pasturing flocks and hunting. They wore no clothing, covering themselves only with the skins of deer and sheep.

Caesar knew this to be true but still he refused to give the Germans a haven. He had undertaken the conquest of Gaul for one purpose only—to create a buffer state between the barbarians of the north and the Italian peninsula. And so he would make no exceptions.

The Germans continued to plead in vain. Then they threatened Caesar. They said that they had only fled from the savages of the north because these people were so strong that even the gods would not dare defy them. But they were not afraid of anyone else and if Caesar would not accept them as friends, then they would be his enemies.

Caesar then brought his legions forward. The Germans were completely unprepared. Men, women and children were camping by their wagons when the Romans suddenly fell upon them. The men at first tried to fight back, but when they saw their terror-stricken women and children being pursued by the Roman cavalry they lost all control. The entire camp, thousands upon thousands, fled in panic toward the Rhine. Here they were overtaken by the Romans and mercilessly slaughtered; some threw themselves into the river and were drowned. None were spared, neither women nor children. Caesar himself records that four hundred and thirty thousand perished that day.

When the news of this massacre reached Rome it caused a great deal of comment. Caesar's enemies said that he had broken all moral bounds and that he should be turned over to the Germans to do with as they liked. They called out against him in the Senate as might have been expected. But his friends, too, were shocked by what had taken place. Even to the brutal Romans of those days, this massacre seemed an appalling thing.

However, Caesar paid no attention to this criticism.

37748

He was determined to show the Germans, once and for all, that Rome would not tolerate their invasions of Gaul and so he decided to carry the war across the Rhine. He did not plan an extensive campaign. He simply wanted to impress the Germans with Roman might. He therefore ordered his men to build a bridge across the Rhine. He could much more easily have used boats to carry his troops across but he knew how deeply such a feat would impress his enemy.

The Roman legionnaires were extremely able workmen and in ten days time they had completed a bridge across the river at the site of modern Bonn. They had cut the timber in the forest, driven piles into the deep, swift waters and built a roadway across—forty feet wide! This is still considered one of the great engineering feats of all time.

Caesar then marched his legions across into the lands of the Germans. And from all parts of the surrounding country the astonished and frightened people sent envoys begging for peace. But Caesar did not accept their surrender too quickly. Master of the situation, he wanted to leave an impression which would not quickly fade. He pursued some of them, sending them fleeing into their dark forests. He burned the villages of others. And at the end of eighteen days, after having gained his purpose, he and his legions returned to Gaul, destroying the bridge behind them.

Caesar's fourth summer was now more than half over. It was the beginning of August, but a few fine weeks still remained. And since all Gaul was quiet and not one tribe stirring, he decided upon an adventure. He decided to cross the channel to visit Britain.

chapter eight

BRITAIN WAS a land of mystery. It lay beyond rough waters and on a clear day its distant white cliffs could be seen from the coast of Gaul.

Caesar wanted to know the size of this land, the names and strength of the main tribes and their military and civil organization. He had repeatedly questioned traders who had been to Britain but they were unable to help him. They knew only about the seacoast.

Caesar realized that it would be a dangerous undertaking to transport a large force across water and land upon a foreign shore, but the spirit of adventure called him. So at Boulogne, he quickly assembled some of the fleet, which on the previous summer had fought the Veneti, and made preparations to embark. In all he had eighty galleys and eighteen barges to transport two legions and a division of cavalry.

On a warm summer evening when the channel was particularly calm, Caesar's armada set sail. It left at midnight and approached the cliffs of Dover at about nine o'clock in the morning. Looking up, the Romans could see a great mass of Britons silhouetted against the sky. They were fully armed. Some were on foot, others on horseback, while still others were in chariots.

Caesar was quick to see that if his ships drew any closer the Britons would hurl spears and rocks down upon his men. And so he ordered his fleet to move up the channel and seek a beach without overhanging cliffs. But as they sailed along, the menacing Britons followed on shore.

At length a place was found. But since the galleys had a large draught they could not be brought too close to the shore and had to be beached in deep water. This meant that the men would be forced to jump into water while fully armed with their heavy packs, weapons and armor. It also meant that standing in the surf, they would make easy targets for the enemy, who could maneuver easily on the beach.

And so when the keels of the Roman vessels finally scraped the bottom, the men were seized with fear and did not jump into the water. All might have been lost had it not been for the standard-bearer of the Tenth Legion. Calling upon the gods, he raised the standard and shouted, "Come, men! Jump, unless you want to betray your standard to the enemy! I, at any rate, shall do my duty to my country and my commander." Then he jumped into the sea and started forward, holding the eagle high in plain view of all.

Seeing this the men cheered wildly and jumped into the surf. But as they had feared, the Britons attacked them fiercely and their cavalry galloped into the waters to surround and slaughter them. The Britons were a wild people and very frightening in appearance. Their faces and hands were dyed blue with the extract from a plant called woad. They had flowing mustaches and were dressed in the skins of wild animals.

However, the Romans fought with their usual courage and discipline, and on reaching the beach they quickly formed battle lines. The legions then attacked and the Britons were forced to retreat. Caesar at once set his men to work building a camp well fortified with dirt walls and a deep ditch.

The next day, while the Romans were still working on their camp, the Britons sent envoys to Caesar asking for peace. They laid the blame for the attack upon the passions of the common people and asked him to forgive their ignorance. Caesar agreed to pardon them and ordered them to bring him hostages. Thus a peace was concluded.

A few days after this, however, a violent storm came up and some of Caesar's ships, which had been left riding at anchor, broke from their moorings and floated out to sea. The rest were dashed one against the other and seriously damaged. Some were beyond repair. And all of the supplies which were stored in them were lost.

The men now felt that all chances of retreat were cut off and they were greatly alarmed. Besides they knew that the Britons would discover their misfortune and would certainly take advantage of it. They feared they would all be killed.

But Caesar remained calm. He at once set men to work repairing the damaged ships. He ordered them to take the boards from twelve vessels that were completely wrecked and repair those that were only partially damaged. And to make up for the lost food supplies he sent foraging parties out into the country. Since it was August, and the grain was ripe, he ordered his men to harvest as much as was needed.

The Britons of course resented having their grain taken, and since the storms had provided them with a good chance to annihilate the Romans, they set aside their promises to Caesar and planned an attack.

So it was that one day a great force of Britons charged a band of Romans who were out gathering grain in the fields. And had Caesar not noticed a great cloud of dust in the distance and guessed what was happening, all would have been killed. He at once sent reinforcements. But the Romans barely escaped, for the fierceness of the attack was such that they could hardly withstand it. They faced a new type of warfare, one which no Romans had ever encountered before. They faced British war chariots. This was something new in the science of war and Caesar was deeply impressed.

He watched with the greatest of interest and made a careful record of this new method of fighting. He described it in these words, "They begin by driving all over the field, hurling javelins; and the terror inspired by the horses and the noise of the wheels is usually enough to throw the enemy ranks into disorder. Then they work their way between their own cavalry units, where the warriors jump down and fight on foot. Meanwhile the drivers retire a short distance from the fighting and station their cars in such a way that the warriors can easily reach them if necessary. In action therefore, they combine the mobility of cavalry with the

staying power of foot soldiers. Their skill may be judged
by the fact that they can control their horses at full
gallop on the steepest incline, check and turn them in a
moment, run along the pole, stand on the yoke and get
back again into the chariot as quick as lightning."

In the days that followed, Caesar's troops and camp
were repeatedly attacked by the British chariots. And
the men became more and more unnerved. But Caesar,
combining cavalry with foot soldiers, was finally able
to check these attacks. Then the wild warriors turned
and beat a quick retreat. The Romans pursued them,
killing many and burning their homes and villages over
a wide area.

It was now the fall of the year and if Caesar had had
a larger force he might have stayed longer in Britain.
But since this was not so, and also because his repaired
ships were not in the best condition, he decided to sail
before the weather changed and the channel became too
rough. And so a few nights later, when the waters were
quiet, the Romans embarked. And after an uneventful
trip, they landed safely on the coast of Gaul the following morning.

Caesar was satisfied with his visit to Britain. It had
been a difficult experience for his troops, but he had
learned some of the things which he wanted to know.
He now knew some of the perils of making a landing
on this foreign shore. He had learned how the Britons
fought in battle and what weapons they used. And above
all, his men now knew how to repulse the attacks of
the wild natives with their blue-painted faces.

These were all things which Caesar was glad to know
because he had secretly decided to return again to Britain

the following summer. This time he planned to take a larger force and invade the country. Now that all Gaul was Roman he felt that it was important for neighboring territories to be aware of Roman might.

And so after settling his legions in winter quarters he gave orders that a great fleet of ships, large enough to carry several legions and divisions of cavalry, should be built during the winter months. These were to be broad in the beam to accommodate more troops and they were to have flat bottoms so that they could be beached close to the shore.

Then Caesar hurried to Cisalpine Gaul to attend to the civil business of his province. While Caesar may have thought lightly of his accomplishments—the bridge across the Rhine and the invasion of Britain, a land so shrouded in mystery that few could believe it really existed — they impressed the people of Rome beyond anything which had ever happened before. They were accustomed to victories but such things as these were like the feats of the gods. Even the Senate was humbled. And it voted Caesar the honor of twenty days of Thanksgiving.

Caesar found his flotilla ready the following spring. There were eight hundred ships, great and small, exactly ten times the number used in his first expedition. Arranging for supplies and organizing his fighting forces, he completed his plans. Then leaving a strong force to watch over Gaul under Labienus, his trusted general, he again sailed for Britain at sunset on the 20th of July, 54 B.C. He commanded five legions as well as two thousand cavalry.

A south wind filled the sails. But after a few hours

it fell and the whole armada was becalmed in mid-channel. At sunrise it was still in the same place. The oars were then brought out and all eight hundred ships had to be rowed the rest of the way. But the soldiers had full confidence in their commander. Besides, those who had been to Britain before had told the others what to expect. They all knew that the blue-faced warriors with their big mustaches and animal skins were no match for Romans. A certain happy spirit of adventure prevailed.

At noon the fleet, still propelled by oars, reached the beach where Caesar's forces had landed the year before. But this time they were not attacked by the Britons. The poor natives, terrified at the vast numbers of ships in which the Romans were approaching, fled into the interior. And so the Romans landed without the least difficulty and quickly set about building a camp.

When the camp was completed Caesar and a great force advanced inland about twelve miles where they met and engaged some Britons in battle. The Romans were victorious and were about to pursue the fleeing Britons when messengers arrived from camp bearing bad news. The south wind which they had welcomed when they set sail had heralded a coming storm. The great Roman armada lay wrecked upon the shore.

Caesar was greatly disturbed at this news, for his fleet was his only bridge with Gaul. Besides, he feared that the Britons would take advantage of the situation, as they had done before. So leaving his army to hold the position which it had just gained, he returned to camp with a small guard. He inspected the wrecked ships and found the damage more than he would have believed possible. Forty vessels were completely destroyed, the rest badly damaged.

Caesar set his best craftsmen to work at once to salvage and repair what they could. He ordered them to work day and night. And everything that could be fished out of the water—planks, masts, ribs, sails, rope —was to be saved. Then he sent a message to Labienus, directing that more ships should be built at once at Boulogne and sent across the channel.

After ten days, and as soon as this gigantic labor was set in motion and the skilled Roman craftsmen understood exactly what was expected, Caesar returned to his troops. And it was fortunate for, just as he feared, the Britons had heard of the disaster and had organized a large force against him.

The chief of a warlike tribe which had its headquarters at St. Albans, about ten miles northwest of modern London, had collected an army of warriors from both sides of the Thames. And when Caesar once more joined his legions they were attacked from every side. The Britons came quickly, struck quickly and left before the slow-moving Roman infantry could engage them. Unlike the Romans, the Britons did not fight in closed formations but spread out, dividing into small mobile units. Thus they could move rapidly from one position to another and send help to any who were being hard pressed. And when Caesar's cavalry pursued one of these units they led them far off into the woods. Here they jumped down from their chariots and attacked on foot.

The Romans were completely unnerved by these tactics, but through sheer tenacity they were finally able to drive the Britons into headlong flight. And after this defeat the Britons never again fought them in a concerted battle. They did, however, entrench themselves on the far side of the Thames. Here they collected large forces and built several lines of defense; they drove great pointed stakes into the earth and river bed at the only point were it could be forded. These they hoped would impede the Romans, but Caesar's cavalry and infantry crossed without hesitation; the men waded across in droves, the water all the way up to their chins. And when the Britons saw the intensity of the Roman courage they fled in every direction.

After this encounter at the Thames and during the rest of Caesar's stay in Briton, his legions were attacked only occasionally. And since Caesar had come to Britain principally to learn about its geography and its people, he did not try to conquer the land. He simply went about noting everything he saw and inquiring about that which was far afield. In this way he learned many things and he wrote them all down.

He found out that Britain was an island and he learned of its dimensions and shape. He learned about Ireland which lay to the west and about the Isle of Man. He was told about the extreme north where there were many small islands and where the winter sun barely rose above the horizon. He discovered that Britain had tin mines and deposits of iron. And through careful measurements and the use of water clocks, he observed that the midsummer nights in Britain were shorter than in southern Gaul and Italy.

Caesar also learned about the people. Those along the coast, he said, had originally migrated from the mainland, but those in the interior seemed to be of very ancient origin. The country was thickly inhabited and the people tended large flocks and herds. They planted their grain without plowing and they did not manufacture even the simplest goods. They lived on meat and milk and dressed in leather and skins. Some, especially near the channel coast, lived in hill forts with walls of earth or rude stone, or in villages of round huts sunk into the ground like those in isolated parts of Gaul. Others lived in caves or in pile dwellings built in marshes. Market centers and town life was just beginning, while gold coins and a currency of iron bars was in use. And to travel along their streams and cross their rivers, the people built small tublike boats out of bent saplings and skins of animals.

Caesar also noted that in contrast to this primitive way of life, the Britons had a special culture. The center of Druidism was in Britain and it was to this place that many of the young men of Gaul came to study for the priesthood. Besides memorizing endless verses and matters of doctrine—for it was forbidden to write down any religious lore—these young men studied astronomy, law, physics and other subjects.

Caesar was the first to reach the shores of Britain and leave a detailed account of his explorations and adventures. And these records proved a great help to another Roman almost a century later. In A.D. 43 the Emperor Claudius again invaded Britain. He conquered the entire land and for the next five hundred years it remained under Roman rule and domination. All this might never have taken place had this country not first been visited by Caesar.

Summer was now ending and Caesar and his forces returned to Gaul. But he had taken so many captives to sell as slaves, living evidence of his expedition, that his fleet had to make two trips across the channel. However, since the weather was fair and the waters calm, both crossings were made without difficulty.

These slaves were the only booty which Caesar was able to send home to Rome as the spoils of his summer campaign. But the Romans, greedy as they were for stolen wealth, did not care. They were awed by what Caesar had accomplished and they talked with the greatest pride and admiration of how he had carried the Roman eagles to this distant land. For a whole century afterward, they still gloried in his feat. Nothing Caesar ever did brought him more fame in Roman eyes.

chapter
nine

WHEN CAESAR returned from his second expedition into Britain, he was forty-six years old. He had already spent four years in Gaul — happy years. They were happy because, for the most part, Caesar had been far removed from the bribery, corruption and political intrigue of Rome. They were also happy years because of his good fortune and unfailing success. He had accomplished what he had set out to do; he had conquered all Gaul from the Pyrenees to the North Sea, from the Atlantic to the Alps. He had brought it under Roman domination and he had subdued and driven back the wild German tribes so that they were no longer a threat to Italy and Rome.

These four years had also been years of energy, of unbroken activity. And now Caesar looked forward to more peaceful times. During the six years which remained of his term, he planned to consolidate Gaul into a Roman province. Then he dreamed of returning to Rome and running for consul a second time.

Now that the Roman Empire was greater than ever before, he wanted to strengthen its government; he dreamed of consolidating all opposing political forces into a rational government. Selfish interests, he felt, must give way to high principles. The government of Rome must no longer serve the corrupt, thirsty for power and wealth; it must serve all the vast peoples of the Empire. The Empire had grown and so he felt that the ideas of government must also change to meet the new conditions.

But just at this time in his life, when everything seemed most hopeful, Caesar encountered the first of a long series of difficulties. From this moment on until the very last day of his life, he faced disappointments and troubles which at times seemed almost insurmountable. And yet he faced them boldly and fought against them. And against all odds and against all difficulties he conquered.

During the years which followed the conference at Lucca, while Caesar was winning new victories in German lands, in Britain and in Gaul, Rome seethed with political unrest. The corrupt senators persisted in their ways. They used every means to gain their ends. They plotted and schemed. They bribed and coerced. They abused their rights as government officials until they had led Rome to the very brink of civil war.

Pompey and Crassus had been elected consuls in 55 B.C. as planned at Lucca and this helped for a while. But then in 53 B.C., after one of the most corrupt elections ever held in Rome, the candidates backed by the evil senators won both consulships.

Bribery and corruption had always played an important part in Roman politics, but during these years it grew to alarming proportions. The entire government was undermined and tottering. And so there were some —even men of sane temperaments—who began to speak of dictatorship as the only answer. And the people felt that the government would not long survive. A crisis seemed imminent.

All of these things might have been prevented if the triumvirate of Caesar, Pompey and Crassus had survived. But destiny played otherwise and these three men were torn apart.

When the consulships of Pompey and Crassus ended in 54 B.C., each received his promised province. Pompey was given Spain and six legions. He chose to stay in Rome and rule it from a distance. But the rich Crassus sought glory. He dreamed of becoming a famous conqueror like Caesar and Pompey and so he hurried off to his alloted province of Syria. From here he planned to launch campaigns which would extend the Roman Empire eastward and carve his name in history. But knowing less about campaigning than did the slaves who worked in his factories in Rome, he set out in high spirits toward disgrace, disaster and death. After some early successes in Palestine, he led his magnificent Roman army across the Euphrates River into the plains of Mesopotamia. It was in the middle of the burning summer. There was no water. Here he died. And with him perished almost every man of his legions, including his son, the brave young officer who had served Caesar so well in Gaul.

With the death of the wealthy Crassus, Caesar and his party lost the backing of a large group of rich men whom he had influenced. They now threw their lot in with the aristocrats. This was a serious loss to the Popular party. But what was far worse was the danger to which Rome was exposed through Crassus' military disaster. The Empire was opened up to invasion from the eastern countries against which Crassus had aimed his campaign.

But the corrupt senators in Rome did not bother with the safety of the Empire. They had a personal grievance which interested them far more. With Crassus dead, they saw a chance of striking out at Caesar and weakening his political position still further. They decided to win Pompey over by promises and flattery. They planned to use him as long as they needed him and then throw him over. They conspired to set the two strongest men of the Empire against each other. Then they would be free to run the government without opposition. They would immediately repeal Caesar's laws and they would do even more, they would recall him in disgrace. He would be tried for treason and impeached!

Such were the plans of the corrupt senators. And it is to Pompey's discredit that he ever listened to their words. However he did not succumb quickly. He fell victim to them only through vanity and a series of uncontrollable events.

For some time past, Pompey had been jealous of Caesar's victories and honors. Although Caesar was his friend and the father of his beloved wife, Julia, he could not control his feelings. Had he not also fought gloriously for the Empire? Had he not been the hero of Rome until Caesar went to Gaul? Now he had been displaced in the people's hearts. He felt he had been cast aside.

Still Pompey might not have succumbed if personal tragedy had not struck both Caesar and him during these years. At this time, Aurelia, Caesar's mother, and Julia, Pompey's wife and Caesar's daughter, both died. And an infant who had been born to Pompey and Julia also died. Thus the bonds which could have held Pompey to Caesar had been severed.

Aurelia and Julia were both women of unusual character and ability. They would certainly have done everything in their power to prevent Pompey from deserting the democratic cause and joining with the traitorous senators. But now that they were gone and he had no one to hold him to the right path, the aristocrats were able to influence him.

The Senatorial party had won the election of 53 B.C. by the basest corruption. Its leaders now determined to continue their control of the government, so they presented two new and carefully chosen candidates for the consulships for the coming year. The Popular party also presented two candidates. Both sides fought desperately to win. And so great was the tension between the two factions that violence finally broke out. There were riots in the Senate as well as on the city streets.

The army, hoping to restore order, suggested that the elections be set aside and that Pompey be declared dictator. But Pompey modestly refused. And so the civil strife continued.

When the time came for voting, the conditions were so bad that the tribunes refused to allow the elections to take place. Thus the year ended. The government officials all went out of office together, leaving the state without any legal officers. And now that there was no state authority to stop them, the supporters of both political parties fought daily in the streets. The city was in a state of revolution.

Now during these days it happened that one of the leaders of the Popular party was murdered by one of the leaders of the Senatorial party. And on the following day, when his body was carried into the Forum by his friends and the people saw what had happened, they felt that the aristocrats had declared an open war against them. They rose in fury and, breaking down the doors of the Senate, they carried in the body of their dead leader. Then they piled up chairs, benches and tables and set fire to the place. The Senate house would be his funeral pyre! His ashes would mingle with the ashes of the Senate itself.

In the hopes of restoring order, Pompey was again offered the dictatorship but once more he refused. He asked, instead, to be named sole consul. And when there was once more a semblance of calm in the city, he announced that he would now choose a second consul to rule with him. Everyone believed he would name Caesar. But the corrupt senators had not wooed Pompey in vain and so he chose one of their friends, a man named

Metellus Scipio. He not only chose him as co-consul but he also married his daughter.

Thus stroke by stroke, while Caesar remained in Gaul, his political future in Rome was weakened. Aurelia, Julia and Crassus were dead. Pompey had deserted him. He was now alone. But he nevertheless looked toward the future without fear. He still dreamed of becoming consul for a second time and establishing an orderly and sound government which would serve the entire Roman Empire.

chapter

ten

THE DIFFICULTIES which had arisen in Rome were not the only difficulties with which Caesar had to contend. His dream of consolidating Gaul into a Roman province was at this time almost shattered. Rumors of civil strife in Rome inspired the people of Gaul to attempt to drive out Caesar and his Roman legions.

In every part of Gaul secret meetings were held, groups of patriots banded together, plans were made and an inspiring leader came to the fore. His name was Vercingetorix (pronounced Vur-sin-jet-o-riks). And this name he engraved in history, for he led one of the most important revolts of all time. He remains to this day one of the greatest heroes of the Gallic people.

Vercingetorix was a young man of a noble family from a south central district now called Auvergne. From birth he had grown up close to the sorrows of his people. He had learned to hate the Romans so intensely that as a youth he was constantly plotting against them.

And his family, fearing the anger of the Romans, finally expelled him from the city of his birth. In this way they hoped to save themselves and the people of their tribe. They also hoped that once an outcast, Vercingetorix would lose his spirit of revolt.

However, Vercingetorix did not change. In fact his exile only served to intensify his feeling. He was highly intelligent and energetic. Realizing that if his people were ever to know freedom they must have a leader, he set about to train himself for the task.

He watched the Roman legions as closely as he could and learned a great deal about supplies, organization, discipline and military leadership. Also knowing that all the past opposition and revolts had come to nothing because the tribes had acted separately, he hoped to organize the whole of Gaul. He therefore wandered about the land seeking out patriots and making friends.

And so it was that during the winter of 53-52 B.C., when all Gaul was inspired by rumors of civil strife in Rome and was dreaming of freedom, a leader came forward.

Since Vercingetorix had been watching the growth of the Gallic discontent, when he was chosen as chief of the great revolt he had a general plan already drawn up—a plan which for surprise and daring was worthy of Caesar himself. Caesar was in Cisalpine Gaul and his legions were all stationed just southwest of Paris. The obvious move was to surround the Roman legions and overwhelm them while preventing Caesar and reinforcements from coming to their aid. To accomplish this, Vercingetorix divided his forces. He stationed one half in southern Gaul to block Caesar's path, while he led the other half northward to attack the Roman legions near Paris.

But Caesar was a master military strategist and a person to whom no difficulty seemed too great. Knowing that if he ordered his legions to come south and join him they would be open to constant and merciless attacks, he decided to force his way through the thick Gallic lines drawn up to stop him.

Leading a few legions that he had quickly assembled in Cisalpine Gaul, he threw them against the passes of the Cévennes Mountains in Auvergne before Vercingetorix's forces knew what had happened. Caesar relates this adventure in the following words, "It was now midwinter. Snow lay thick on the Cévennes . . . and all passes were blocked. Yet my troops accomplished the unbelievable feat of cutting a road through drifts up to six feet deep and thereby enabled us to get through. The rebels were taken by surprise. They believed the Cévennes as good a fortification as any wall. At that time of the year, in fact, the range was considered impassable even for single travelers."

As soon as the Romans had come over the snow-covered mountains, Caesar ordered them to spread through the country and to do everything possible to terrorize the population. They burned homes, killed and destroyed everything they touched. The natives at once sent messengers to Vercingetorix, begging him to come to their help. And the rebel leader turned back, abandoning his plan for attacking the legions in the North. He thought that he could return to this later; first he would annihilate the Romans in the South. He might even capture Caesar himself.

This change in Vercingetorix' plans was exactly what Caesar had hoped for. Secretly leaving his troops under the command of Decimus Brutus, the same young officer who had directed the sea battle against the Veneti, he rushed north on horseback with a few companions. He took a roundabout route in order to pass unnoticed. He rode night and day, joining his legions south of Paris, two hundred miles away, before Vercingetorix ever suspected that he was not still in Auvergne.

Once more at the head of his legions, Caesar started in pursuit of Vercingetorix. He marched southward, taking three towns on the way, until he came to the city of Bourges which was about one hundred and twenty-five miles directly south of Paris. Here he halted.

Bourges was the finest and most strongly fortified city in all Gaul. Its destruction, he knew, would strike a hard blow at the heart of the Gauls. They were an emotional people and easily discouraged. Such a defeat might even lead to Vercingetorix's surrender.

The walls of Bourges were built of alternate layers of stone and timber and were forty feet thick and eighty feet high. They could not be burnt or penetrated with battering rams. It was therefore believed by the Gauls that Bourges was inpregnable. But the people of Gaul still did not know the full temper and capabilities of the Romans, and they failed to appreciate the skill of their engineers.

Caesar decided to build a large ramp of turf and wood that would reach to the top of the city wall. It was to be several yards wide. Using this ramp, the Romans would then be able to pour their troops into the city. And so during four long weeks, in winter cold and rain, while the city was besieged the Roman engineers and soldiers labored.

During this time the Romans suffered terribly, for besides besieging the city and building the ramp, they were also set upon from the rear. With a large force, Vercingetorix had drawn near and was cutting off their supplies. He was in fact so successful that he nearly starved them out. He burnt all the near-by granaries, leaving the Romans without bread for many days. And since the Gauls had hidden their cattle in the deep forests, they were also without meat.

At length the Romans were faced with actual famine but not one man uttered a word of complaint. And when Caesar addressed his men and said he was ready to call off the siege if they wanted him to, they all insisted on fighting on. The ramp was nearly finished. Victory was not far off. "To give up at such a time," they said, "would be unworthy of Romans."

And so they fought on under the most dreadful conditions. But when in time the ramp was finished, they were rewarded for their courage. Caesar gave the signal for assault. His main force rushed up to the top of the ramp and swarmed over the walls, while other troops guarded the gates so that none could escape from the city. Maddened by starvation, the Romans spared neither man, woman nor child. Out of a population of forty thousand people only eight hundred survived.

The proud city of Bourges fell to the Romans, but the Gauls and Vercingetorix did not surrender as Caesar had thought they might. In fact the loss of this city seemed only to unite the Gauls all the more and they rallied behind Vercingetorix with greater enthusiasm than before.

In Vercingetorix, Caesar had to deal with a very different man from any he had ever met. The spirit and courage which he instilled in his people was such that they were willing to sacrifice anything to follow him. And Caesar quickly learned that the Gauls would not easily give up their fight. Their dream of freedom was strong. Wherever he and his legions went they found that the people had burned their farms, their granaries, their towns, rather than surrender them. Sometimes at night the entire horizon was lighted by a ring of blazing fires!

But Caesar was determined to subdue all Gaul and make it into a Roman province. And so he sought out Vercingetorix at every chance and engaged him in battle. However, during one of these battles he and his legions were badly defeated. They were besieging the city of Gergovia, in Auvergne, when the Gauls attacked them in such numbers that they were nearly surrounded and Caesar himself only barely escaped being captured. He lost forty-seven officers and hundreds of men. And it must be noted that this was the only defeat the Romans ever suffered in Gaul while Caesar was leading his men on the field.

Never before had Caesar's position been at a lower ebb. Not only had he suffered a smashing defeat but he now heard that four legions, which he had sent toward Paris under the command of Labienus, were in serious difficulties. At this moment all his conquests in Gaul — eight years of campaigns — seemed wholly undone! It was imperative that he go at once to the aid of Labienus, if his legions were not to be annihilated. And so regardless of the danger, he gave the order for his weakened forces to march forward. And strangely enough, his position improved from that moment on.

But the Gauls had been fired by their great victory at Gergovia and were now more set in their purpose than ever before. Their warriors swore a solemn oath that they would not return to their wives and children until they had ridden twice through the Roman army. And with this vow on their lips they fought the Romans with even greater courage and daring than they had displayed in the past.

It was with this fervor that one day they met Caesar's legions in open combat on a broad plain in eastern Gaul. But although their courage was unequaled, they lacked the discipline and organization of the Roman legions. And so in spite of all their vows, the Gauls were badly defeated and instead of riding twice through the Roman army, they themselves were ridden over and hewn down by Caesar's ruthless horsemen.

Vercingetorix and his entire army were sent flying for fifty miles over the hills. Caesar pressed close behind, driving him and his eighty thousand men into the neighboring fortress of Alesia. And it was here that in the days that followed, one of the most remarkable sieges of all military history took place.

Alesia is situated on the flat top of a round hill, the slopes of which are very steep. This hill rises from a narrow plain which lies between two small rivers which provide an extraordinary defense.

To attack Vercingetorix in this position was quite

impossible. But Caesar felt that he could blockade him, surround him and starve him into surrender. If this plan worked, then Vercingetorix himself would be captured and the war would come to a sudden end.

Caesar at once set his legions to work to surround the entire area with fortifications. They began cutting trenches, building walls, establishing camps and constructing blockhouses. Not content with all this, the Romans then took possession of all the surrounding hills so that they could establish watchtowers.

For a time Vercingetorix watched this Roman activity without fully understanding the underlying plan. But when he recognized the danger, he made several attempts to break out of the encircling trap before it was completely closed. However, each attempt failed. And realizing that his one hope now lay in getting help from outside, he sent forth some messengers on horseback.

It was only through the most amazing valor that a few of these managed to break through the Roman lines. Once past the enemy, they rode with all possible speed into every district of Gaul to rouse the people and to organize new forces to come to the rescue. "Vercingetorix and his men have food for only thirty days!" they cried. "If you do not want to betray him and the cause of liberty you must come at once!"

The critical moment in the Gallic war for freedom had arrived. It was now a matter of life or death, liberty or bondage.

And at every crossroad in Gaul the people answered the call. Bands of patriots formed and started marching toward Alesia. And as they marched along, gathering strength as one group joined another, they formulated a plan to surround Caesar's forces and squeeze them between their two armies; their new Gallic forces would press from the outside while Vercingetorix's forces would press from the inside. In such a nutcracker movement they hoped they would annihilate all the hated Roman legions at one time.

Caesar was not yet aware of this approaching army. And day after day while Vercingetorix and his men looked down helplessly from the heights of Alesia, the Romans continued building their encircling web. Like long lines of ants they worked steadily, all day, all night, without rest, digging, carrying, building. They built twenty-three forts one third of a mile apart. They dug a double trench the circumference of which measured a full eight miles. On the western side of the plain, at the base of Alesia, it was twenty feet deep with almost perpendicular sides. This was the work of the Roman soldiers following the plans of the Roman engineers. These engineers were the same men who had directed the building of the ramp at Bourges and the bridge across the Rhine. And these fortifications, designed by them, made up the most gigantic trap the world had yet seen.

News now reached Caesar that a quarter of a million Gauls were on their way to save the besieged patriots at Alesia. He also learned of the plan to crush his army in a great pincer movement. At this moment Caesar could safely have withdrawn his forces. But instead he decided to hold his position. And so when the first line of fortifications was barely finished, his men had to turn around and construct an outer line of defense on the same huge scale. This new line was further strengthened by areas of staked pitfalls, barbed spikes and other treacherous Roman contrivances.

When this new line was finished the Roman forces occupied a position unique in all military history. They were hemmed in between two circular lines of defense with the enemy surrounding them on all sides. It was not an enviable position, especially since they were so far outnumbered by the Gauls. But time helped Caesar's forces, for those besieged in Alesia had already exhausted their food supply and were weakened by famine. However, starved as they were they gathered strength when, from the heights, they saw in the distance a great dust cloud and then a host with glittering lances and flying banners which was coming to their rescue.

A few hours later the three armies were ready for the last terrible struggle. Every Gaul knew that defeat meant destruction and centuries of bondage. Every Roman knew that victory would put an end to his superhuman labors. With victory he could rest — and the serpent of revolt would never stir again. Gaul would this time remain conquered.

Climbing to an elevated place where he could look down over a broad area, Caesar at last gave the command for action. The clash came with terrific fury. On this first day the fighting lasted from noon until nightfall. The Romans were attacked simultaneously from front and rear but they were able to withstand all the assaults, and with darkness Vercingetorix drew back sadly to the heights of Alesia.

However, the new Gallic army did not rest. After the

fighting had stopped they built ladders to scale the walls of the fortifications and then spread out over the countryside, gathering logs and rocks with which to fill up the Roman trenches. And at midnight they began a second attack.

Vercingetorix, hearing the battle cries, sensed what was happening and again attacked the Romans. But Caesar's army was too highly trained. Every man had his post. The javelins, slings, crossbows and catapults were all at hand. And so the Romans were able to fight back, inflicting great losses on the Gauls. Besides, the Gauls got caught in the areas of staked pits and barbed spikes and fell in heaps, easy prey for Roman javelins and arrows. After only a few hours the Gauls were forced to abandon the battle. A young Roman officer named Mark Antony was one of the heroes of this night.

The next day the Gauls tried a different tactic. They decided on a surprise attack from the heights. And so at dawn sixty thousand Gauls from the outer circle secretly stole away into the hills where they lay concealed until noon. Then they suddenly swooped down on the Romans. This was the signal for a concerted effort by all the Gauls. Vercingetorix' forces attacked on every side of the inner circle. The other Gauls attacked on the outer circle. Thus the Romans were under fierce pressure at every conceivable point. And in one section they began to weaken and draw back.

But Caesar, seeing this from his lookout post, sent Labienus forward with a large force. However, Vercingetorix also threw in more forces and so the Romans were not able to stem the breach. Caesar threw in still more men. The fighting grew desperate and, realizing how hard pressed his men were, Caesar left his outpost and rode down into their midst. In his scarlet cloak and bareheaded, he mingled with his soldiers and urged them on. His presence always inspired the men and so now they threw away their arrows and rushed upon the Gauls with drawn swords.

While his men were holding the Gauls in hand to hand combat, Caesar sent a few detachments of cavalry into the same hills from which the Gauls had launched their surprise attack that morning. They suddenly raced down and the Gauls, taken by surprise, were thrown into confusion and hacked to pieces. Thousands fell dead. In this encounter seventy-four standards were captured by the Romans.

Seeing this, Vercingetorix drew his men back into Alesia. And the vast host that had come to his rescue lost heart and began streaming out over the countryside. Caesar's cavalry pursued, slaughtering and capturing them by the thousands.

By sundown of this day one of the most daring exploits of all military history was over. A Roman army of approximately fifty thousand men had defeated an enemy of about three hundred and thirty thousand, an enemy which had completely surrounded it on all sides.

After a long tragic night and with the coming light of day, Vercingetorix called a council of his officers. He stood before them and spoke. "It was not for selfish ends that I embarked on this war. What I did, I did for my country. But now I must bow to the decrees of Fate. My task is done. And I offer myself as a victim. Kill me and send my head to Caesar; or if you like deliver me to him alive."

The Gauls on the heights of Alesia, starving and hopeless, were forced to accept unconditional surrender. And Vercingetorix and his chiefs came down the steep hillside into the Roman camp.

Dressed in his brilliant scarlet cloak, Caesar sat on an embankment before his camp while one by one the high officers of the defeated Gauls were brought before him. They gave up their weapons and became captives. Then Vercingetorix rode forward on his horse. He dismounted. And placing his sword at Caesar's feet he knelt and was made a prisoner.

After this, and with Vercingetorix standing there in chains, long lines of the defeated Gauls were marched before the victorious Caesar. And as they passed they threw their weapons into a great pile. The whole army became prisoners of war, and most of them were sold to the slave contractors to be sent to Rome.

While Caesar sold most of the war captives of Alesia into slavery, he did not punish the civilian population of Gaul. He knew that the wounds received in war could only be healed by generous treatment. And since his purpose was not to enslave the Gauls but to bring them into the Roman Empire, and in time give them the privileges of Roman citizens, he did everything he could to erase the memory of defeat.

In fact, Caesar's desire for this was so strong that he spent the entire last year of his term in organizing the government of the new province and making friends of the people and their leaders. By the generosity of his plans he proved to the Gauls that to be members of the Roman Empire would be of great benefit to them and their country. And so they were contented and resolved to live in peace from that time on. In the years that followed they never wavered from this purpose.

Thus it was that the Gauls joined the Roman Empire and gave up all dreams of freedom. But they did not forget Vercingetorix, their great leader and hero. Through the centuries which followed, the story of his noble fight and tragic death was handed down by one generation to another. Little children learned from their elders how he had led their forefathers at Bourges, Gergovia and Alesia; how he had finally been forced to surrender and how he had been taken to Rome and cast in a dungeon. Here he was held in chains for six years and then marched in Caesar's Triumph. After which he was strangled in a dungeon deep beneath the Temple of Jupiter while Caesar was above offering thanks to the gods.

This is the story which was told to Gallic children generation after generation. And nineteen centuries after the death of noble Vercingetorix, his countrymen, the French, now long free from Roman bondage, erected a monument to his memory. It stands today on the hill at Alesia where his last great battle took place.

*chapter
eleven*

WHILE CAESAR was busy organizing the government of Gaul, his enemies in Rome continued to plot against him. But they did not quite know how to deal with him, for he was so popular that they feared a general uprising if they should harm him openly.

After Caesar's victory over Vercingetorix, the Senate had been forced against its will to give him another Thanksgiving. They thought twenty days would be ample but the people brushed their opinion aside and honored their hero with sixty full days intsead. All over Italy the altars smoked with offerings and crowds of worshipers prayed to the immortal gods to bless and protect the greatest Roman of all. And in certain Cisalpine towns the people strewed Caesar's path with flowers. Such demostrations of favor were enough to strike fear into the blackest senatorial heart. And although the evil senators longed to use violent measures, they decided to handle the situation in some other fashion.

Caesar's ten-year term in Gaul and Cisalpine Gaul was to expire at the end of 49 B.C. Under Pompey's consulship, a few years before, Caesar had been officially promised the right to run for consul in 48 B.C. while still with his troops in Cisalpine Gaul. And although this promise had been immediately nullified by another law, still the senators feared that Caesar and his friends might insist upon its recognition. And the people, they knew, would support such a move.

So they searched Caesar's record to find cause to impeach him but they were disappointed. His wars in Gaul had not cost Rome a cent; they had paid their own way. He had doubled his soldiers' pay and his military chests were bursting with wealth. He had sent thousands upon thousands of slaves back to Italy and at his own expense he had built several beautiful buildings to adorn the Forum. Alone he had added a vast new province to the Empire, a province larger than Spain. And the Gauls whom he had conquered were now friendly and co-operative with Rome. Besides, they were devoted friends of their conqueror!

Such were the facts which Caesar's record revealed. But his enemies were determined to have their way. And so they took the law into their own hands. Having by this time completely won over Pompey, they gave him two legions with which to enforce their wishes. Then in a highhanded manner they threw out the duly elected consuls and replaced them with two men of their own choice.

With the government thus secured in their own hands they recalled Caesar. They announced that a mistake had been made concerning the expiration date of his term of office. They said that by the new calculations—the correct calculations—his term would end six months sooner than he had thought. He would therefore have to come home before running for consul.

This was a scheme to ruin Caesar. If he accepted the new and false calculations, gave up his troops and returned to Rome as a private citizen, he would fall easy prey to their evil plans. They could then invent charges against him and impeach him or otherwise prevent his election. If, on the other hand, he refused to accept the new calculations and remained with his armies, he would be held in contempt of the Senate.

However, since Caesar understood only too clearly what his enemies were trying to do, he wrote to the Senate suggesting three very reasonable alternatives. But when this letter was introduced in the Senate, Caesar's enemies tried to prevent it from being read. Failing in this they forbade a debate concerning it. Caesar's friends fought hard but with Pompey and his troops ready to use force if necessary to strengthen the hand of the evil senators, all their efforts failed. And an order was issued that Caesar must dismiss his army before a certain day; failing to do this he would be considered an enemy of the state.

Two of the people's tribunes, Mark Antony and Cassius Longinus, vetoed this act, but the senators disregarded their constitutional power. They then officially suspended the government, gave their two hand-picked consuls absolute power and declared martial law. A conscription was called throughout Italy and Pompey was made commander-in-chief with headquarters at Capua. The people's tribunes fled.

All this was accomplished in less than a week. The

corrupt senators, pretending to defend the Republic, had finally destroyed it completely. It amounted to an open declaration of war against the people.

When this news reached Caesar where he was staying at Ravenna, close to the Adriatic in Cisalpine Gaul, he at once understood the seriousness of the situation. He did not waver, but instead made a bold decision. Calling together the men of his Thirteenth Legion, the only legion he had with him, since he had left all the others in Gaul, he spoke to them. These were only a few of his soldiers but they represented all the rest.

He told them everything that had happened in Rome and he reminded them that for nine years, under his leadership, they had served their country with honor and distinction. He told them how the aristocrats had won over Pompey, for whom he had always shown the greatest love and respect, and how they had given him command of an Italian army. Such an act was strictly against Roman law. In the past such measures had been taken only to restore order in times of revolution. The law had not only been violated, it had been completely cast aside, while the veto power of the tribunes, the people's true representatives, had been declared null and void. Then Caesar concluded, "All this time I have suffered a long series of injustices at the hands of my enemies in Rome who are determined to destroy my good name." And he called upon his men to defend his honor and reputation.

The men cheered wildly in reply. They swore to stand by him and to defend the tribunes and the democratic ideals of the Republic. In their fervor they volunteered to serve without pay and many came forward offering what money and possessions they had as contributions for the expenses of the coming civil war.

There was only one man who deserted Caesar at this time. He was his most trusted general—Labienus. Caesar had previously been warned that Pompey and the aristocrats in Rome were trying to win over Labienus, but he had refused to believe these reports. However, he now found that Labienus had betrayed his trust and friendship. He stole away without telling anyone and hurried to join Pompey in southern Italy, leaving all his belongings behind. Caesar had them carefully packed and sent after him. Thus ended a long, close friendship.

But Caesar could not brood over his loss. He had pressing matters to attend to. With the loyalty of his Thirteenth Legion assured, he now sent for several other legions from Gaul to join him as soon as possible. Then without further delay he started out for the city of Rimini. This city is on the Adriatic just south of Ravenna and was the first Italian city beyond the border of Caesar's province.

Now it was a strict Roman law that the governor of a province could not cross over the border of his territory with his troops. Such an act was considered high treason and was punishable by death. But Caesar, holding the survival of Rome dearer than life itself, led his Thirteenh Legion forward. He had only five thousand men with him but he knew that his other legions were completely devoted to him and would join him without delay. And so he pushed on toward Rimini.

A little river called the Rubicon marked the boundary of Caesar's province. He and his men reached this point late at night. For a moment he stood upon the bank, then

gave the order to advance. They marched forward.
There was now no possibility of turning back. Caesar
had crossed the Rubicon.

When the news reached Rome that Caesar had crossed
the boundary of his province and was in the city of Rimini, a wild panic seized his enemies. The fact that he had
only five thousand men with him at that moment did not
lessen their fears. Their guilt took complete possession
of them and they could think only of flight.

And so they fled from Rome. They fled in terror. Consuls, senators, public officers, politicans and everyone
else connected with the corrupt, intriguing senators left
Rome. They abandoned their wives, children, estates and
wealth. They did not even take the Treasury funds. They
left the city on foot, in carriages, on horseback and in
litters and chariots. And oddly enough, Cicero, the greatest orator of Rome and Caesar's boyhood friend, was
among them.

Some sought refuge in the country and in neighboring
towns and cities, but most rushed southward to Capua
to seek the protection of Pompey and his two legions.
Here, bolstered by the soldiers and the promise of a
larger army which they believed was being recruited all
over Italy, their spirits began to revive. They held con-
ferences and sent envoys to Caesar urging him to listen
to reason. Using Pompey's name they appealed to him to
negiotate with them. However, their words were false;
they were only seeking time.

Caesar was not deceived by Pompey's appeal. But
wishing sincerely to avoid war, he used this opportunity
to try to find a solution. He sent back a message in which
he stated very clearly all the injustices which his enemies

had practiced against him. He reminded them of all their evil schemes and acts, one by one. Yet, he said, he was willing to make peace. "Let both sides disarm in order to allow the government to operate without the threat of terrorism," he said. "If this is done, then I will give up every point in dispute."

He then described in detail what he felt should be done. He proposed that he and Pompey should simultaneously dismiss their troops. Pompey should then go to Spain and attend to his duties as governor, while he would return to Rome as a private citizen. At the same time, the government should be reinstated and free elections should be held. Caesar also suggested that a personal interview between Pompey and himself might be helpful.

When these proposals were discussed by Pompey and his scheming friends, there were some among them who said that Caesar's words were definitely fair and that his suggestions should be accepted. But there were a few who were still defiant. They were set against democratic government and they held Pompey in their power. And in the end their opinion won out. Therefore, while half promising that at some future date Pompey would go to Spain and that the government would be restored, they ordered Caesar to evacuate Rimini at once and return to his province.

Caesar knew that these promises were false and in reply he now began marching toward Rome. Every town and city he came to opened its gates and welcomed him.

Although these were difficult days for Caesar, he tried to make peace with his enemies. He wrote to Pompey reminding him of their past friendship and asking him to reconsider his actions and to think first of the welfare of the Empire. He also wrote to Cicero. He knew that Cicero had long ago deserted him and had joined his enemies in the Senate and he begged him to return to the right path. He promised to forgive all those who had plotted against him. In one remarkable letter, which has fortunately been preserved, he frankly discloses his plans, plans which were very different from those of all previous conquerors. "My method of conquest shall be a new one; I will fortify myself with compassion and generosity."

However, neither Pompey nor Cicero would listen to Caesar's pleas. They preferred to continue their alliance with the corrupt senators.

But as Caesar advanced closer and closer to Rome, Pompey and his friends became more desperate. And from two of Cicero's letters to friends written at this time, we get a picture of the confusion and indecision which ruled the camp of the aristocrats at Capua. "You ask what Pompey means to do," Cicero writes. "I do not think he knows himself. . . . It is all panic and blunder. We are not certain whether he will make a stand or leave Italy. If he stays I fear his army is too unreliable." In the second letter he writes, "The consuls are helpless. The draft of recruits for the army has failed. . . . With Caesar pressing forward, and our general [Pompey] doing nothing, men will not volunteer. . . . Pompey is miserable and, incredible though it be, is prostrate. He has no courage, no purpose, no force, no energy. . . . He orders the consuls to go to Rome and bring away the money from the Treasury. How are they to go without an escort, or how return? . . ."

But if Pompey did not know what to do, Caesar did.

With his usual decision and swiftness he pushed on toward Rome. And as he had written to Cicero, he fortified himself with "compassion and generosity." Everywhere he went he won friends. Even those towns and people who favored Pompey's forces were won over. And many joined Caesar's army. By the time he was within two or three days march of Rome his forces had swelled to thirty thousand.

However, the sincerity of Caesar's words to Cicero was best illustrated at Corfinium where he met and conquered some of Pompey's followers. A group of young aristocrats, who had grown desperate by Pompey's inactions, had joined together in the hope of stopping Caesar's advance. They had raised a force of recruits which numbered a few thousand at the most. Caesar easily surrounded and overwhelmed this force. He thus held in his hands the sons and relatives of many of his most bitter enemies. But he did not order them to be made prisoners or killed. He was satisfied simply to speak to them. Then he forgave them, even the leaders, and allowed all to go free. As a result, the majority of the rank and file and some of the young leaders joined him and swore allegiance to his cause.

The capture of Corfinium and the desertion of Pompey's followers to Caesar caused a second panic among the senatorial forces at Capua. They again thought only of flight. They felt that if they could escape across the Adriatic they could muster a powerful force and then return and fight Caesar some other day. And so, with Pompey leading them, they hurried to Brindisi where ships were waiting for them. Pompey and his two legions, over half the senators from Rome and numberless hangers-on, ran for their lives.

But they need not have been so terrified, for Caesar was a most reasonable man. And guessing that they would flee, he wrote to many of them assuring them of his wish for peace. He again begged Pompey to return to Rome as his friend and to work with him for the good of the country as they had done in the past. And to Cicero he wrote that he would be content to step down and live under Pompey's rule if he could be guaranteed that his life would be spared!

But this was a time in history when society was sick with an illness bred of corruption and fear. It was a time when men would not listen to reason. And so Pompey and his friends turned a deaf ear to Caesar's pleas and ran away. Only one from their midst turned back toward Rome. He was Cicero.

But Cicero was a man of vacillating character. He always sought to join the winning side. From some of his letters we learn of his thoughts at this time. "My connections, personal and political, attach me to Pompey. . . . Yet Caesar shows in many ways that he wishes me well. . . . Still ought I to expose myself to the danger and perhaps disgrace which would lie before me, should Pompey come back into power?" In another letter he said, "I saw from the first that Pompey only thought of flight; if I now follow him, where shall we go? . . . Oh, most perplexing position!" These were some of Cicero's thoughts at this time. And so he finally decided to abandon Pompey and rejoin his friend, the victorious Caesar. How-

ever, he rejoined Caesar with many reservations in his
mind. From still another letter we learn his treacherous
thoughts. "Caesar," he wrote, "is but mortal. There are
many ways in which he can be got rid of."

Caesar was pleased at Cicero's return. But this did not
solve any of his problems. Pompey had escaped. To follow him at once was not possible, for there were not
enough transports. And to remain in Italy was too dangerous. Caesar knew that Pompey would at once raise a
great army in the East. In the West, in Spain, he already
had a large number of Roman legions under the command of able and loyal generals. Thus it was that if Caesar and his troops remained in Italy they would find
themselves between Pompey's two great armies.

Caesar understood the danger of his position. And
with his characteristic clarity of thought, vision and directness, he at once decided upon a plan. He would re-
organize the government in Rome as swiftly and as well
as he could and then go to Spain and conquer Pompey's
legions. With this threat from the West eliminated, he
would then be free to meet Pompey's forces in the East
and bring the Civil War to an end.

Arriving in Rome, the city which he had not seen in
ten long years, he at once took command. He sent forces
to occupy Sicily and Sardinia upon which Rome depended
for its grain, then called together all the members of the
Senate who had not fled.

When they were assembled he spoke to them. He said
that he had never asked for extraordinary honors. He
had fulfilled his term in Gaul and Cisalpine Gaul and had
waited the full ten years required by law before running

for consul a second time. A promise which had been given him by the government had been broken. Then he spoke of his patience, of the concessions which he had offered and of his unjust recall by the Senate and the suppression of the rights of the tribunes, Mark Antony and Cassius Longinus. He had always sought peace, he said. He had repeatedly asked his enemies for interviews, but all in vain.

Then Caesar asked the assembled senators to put aside what differences they might have and unite in an effort to form a new government. Caesar has recorded the sense of this plea in the following words, "I pressed them to assume the reins of government and to co-operate with me in its administration. I told them, however, that if they feared to undertake these duties, I would save them any embarrassment by taking full responsibility myself." He then advised the senators to send envoys to Pompey to discuss conciliation. And he concluded with these words, "It has been my endeavor to excel as a man of action; I wish now to prove that I am second to none in a sense of justice and of equity."

The senators all approved of sending envoys of peace to Pompey, but since Pompey had declared before leaving that any senator who remained in Rome would be considered an enemy of the state, none dared to go. For three long days they discussed the problem and finally Caesar came to the conclusion that with such indecisive people nothing could be accomplished; peace could be gained only by the sword. So he asked the Assembly of the people for money to fight Pompey and they voted him the funds in the Treasury. Then appointing a governor to rule Rome during his absence and leaving Mark Antony in command of an army of occupation, he returned to Gaul to prepare for his attack against Pompey's forces in Spain.

Leading several of his legions from Gaul, Caesar hurried across the Pyrenees, determined to complete the Spanish campaign as quickly as possible. He knew that a long war in Spain would be fatal. It would give Pompey the opportunity to return to Italy without anyone to oppose him.

However, Caesar's campaign in Spain was not won too easily. Bad weather and other difficulties caused him serious reverses. At one time news reached Rome that he had been forced to surrender. And Cicero, along with others who liked to be with the winning side, hurried down to Brindisi and crossed over the sea to join Pompey.

But the rumor proved to be false. A military leader of Caesar's ability was not to beaten quite so quickly. And exactly forty days after Caesar first engaged Pompey's Spanish legions, all Spain lay at his feet.

After this campaign, Caesar forgave all his enemies— officers and men alike—just as he had while on his march from Rimini to Rome. Even though some were found to be young nobles whom he had previously pardoned and released at Corfinium, he took no prisoners, imposed no death penalties. He asked only that Pompey's defeated legions swear not to bear arms against him in the future. He kept his word; "My method of conquest shall be a new one; I will fortify myself with compassion and generosity."

And on the whole, his new method of conquest served him well. The mass of men and officers kept their promise. But there were some who joined Pompey. They lived to fight Caesar again.

With the Spanish campaign at an end Caesar returned to Rome, bringing his legions with him. He was now ready to face Pompey in the East.

chapter
twelve

Returning to Rome, Caesar found that during his absence he had been named dictator by a vote of the people for the sole purpose of ordering new elections. This he did. And he was himself elected consul with a friend as co-consul. In this way did he receive the office he had desired for so long.

But Caesar was not as happy as he might have been because his one dream had always been the expansion and strengthening of the Roman Empire. But now because of the conflict between his democratic beliefs and the selfish and reactionary beliefs of his enemies, Rome was torn by civil war. The Empire was divided in half; he controlled the western part while Pompey held the eastern half. A violent struggle seemed inevitable. Both he and Pompey were great generals, masters of the science of war, and Caesar knew that this would be a life-and-death struggle.

While Caesar was in Spain, Pompey had organized a

large force at Durazzo directly across the Adriatic from
Brindisi. He now had both an army and a fleet. And over
the whole of Italy there hung the fear of invasion. Caesar
felt that he could not waste a moment's time, for if Pompey were to return then the war would lay waste Italian
soil. He was anxious to leave at once to engage Pompey,
but the civil affairs of Rome and Italy were in such a
wild state that he was forced to wait a few days and
attempt to bring a certain amount of order out of the
chaos.

Risking the loss of the support of the people by dis-
appointing their hopes of far-reaching reforms, Caesar
attended only to the most pressing problems. During the
year which had passed since he had crossed the Rubicon
and the evil senators had fled in terror, public credit had
been shaken. Debts had not been paid, money lenders had
taken matters into their own greedy hands and were
charging usurious rates. Caesar therefore attended to
these problems first, passing certain regulations and con-
trols. He then directed the proper officers to review the
cases of all who claimed that they had been unjustly
treated in the courts during Pompey's days in power,
and recalled a great number of people who had been
exiled by Pompey and his senatorial friends.

Caesar was so pressed for time that he was unable to
give his attention to many other problems and he asked
the people to be patient, promising that when he returned
he would see that justice was done for all. However, he
did find time during these crowded days to fulfill a promise which he had made many years before. He granted
full citizenship to all the free and loyal inhabitants of
southern Gaul. He had always felt that a conquered peo-

ple should have a voice in the government which ruled them. And so from this time on Gaul was represented in Rome; representatives chosen by the Gauls now became members of the Senate.

Caesar accomplished all these things in exactly eleven days. At the end of this time he and his army left Rome and headed for Brindisi. He started out with twelve legions, but the long forced marches and the sudden change from the dry climate of Gaul and Spain to the damp autumn weather of southern Italy drained the health of his soldiers. Many became ill and had to drop out of the ranks. Because of this he had only thirty thousand men when he reached Brindisi.

This was, of course, a dangerously small army to undertake the great task that lay ahead. And Ceasar's position was further jeopardized by the fact that he did not have enough transports to convey all his men at one time. Two trips would be necessary. And both of these trips would have to be made under the constant threat of attacks by Pompey's fleet.

However, this did not stop Caesar, and with half of his troops he sailed from Brindisi. After a rough but swift crossing, he landed safely on the far shore about fifty miles south of Pompey's main force at Durazzo.

Caesar then ordered his transports to return immediately to Brindisi, under the cover of darkness, and pick up the rest of his troops which he had left under the command of his loyal officer Mark Antony. In the meantime he and his forces began moving toward Durazzo.

The transports did not start out during the night as Caesar had ordered and so they were sighted by Pompey's fleet and thirty were captured. But what proved still worse was that Pompey's fleet now blockaded Brindisi and thus prevented Mark Antony from setting sail. Day after day he waited in vain for a chance to break through and join Caesar.

By this time Caesar had reached the outskirts of Durazzo. He ordered that a camp be built and fortifications set up, fully believing that Mark Antony and the rest of his men were following behind and would join him in a day or two at the most.

However, while preparing for battle Caesar did not abandon hopes of peace and once more sent a message to Pompey. "It is our common duty to make concessions and put an end to hostilities," he said. "We should consider the unhappy plight of our country. . . . Now is the only time to negotiate peace, when each of us feels confident of his own strength, and each can feel himself the other's equal. If one of us gains any substantial advantage he will believe himself to have the upper hand and will reject any suggestion of give and take; he will never be content with a division of authority when supreme power seems within his grasp. Because of our failure in the past to reach an agreement the decision should lie with the Senate and the people at Rome. Meanwhile . . . we should publicly swear to disband our legions within three days."

These were most reasonable words. But Pompey did not even read them to the end. Influenced by Labienus who was now one of Caesar's most violent enemies, he said, "What care I for life or country if I am to hold both by the favor of Caesar? How can I make peace now? Men will say that Caesar has brought me back to Italy."

However, the soldiers of both camps disagreed with Pompey and Labienus. Since armies were divided only by a small river, men fraternized with each other and asked why this war had been undertaken in the first place. And because the common soldiers all idolized Caesar, they called a meeting to see if some agreement could be reached. Pompey and Labienus, of course, opposed this meeting, but not daring to stop it they pretended to co-operate. Labienus planted some traitors in among the men and suddenly, in the middle of the discussions, one of Caesar's officers was attacked with a shower of arrows. His men tried to protect him. Many were wounded and the meeting broke up in the wildest confusion, with Labienus shouting, "There can be no peace until you bring us Caesar's head!"

At last, after many long weeks of waiting, Antony was able to break through the blockade. And Caesar with his entire force now united was ready and eager for battle.

But in the fight which followed, Caesar's forces suffered defeat. Nearly one thousand of his soldiers were killed, thirty-two standards were lost and several hundred men were taken. These prisoners were turned over to Labienus who paraded them up and down while taunting them with jibes and calling them "old comrades." Then they were brutally killed.

The disgrace of this defeat only served to steel the fighting spirit of Caesar's men. They wanted to attack again immediately, but Caesar spoke to them calmly and explained that it would be much wiser to wait until some later time. He praised them for their courage, reminded them of all their past victories and promised to lead them to further glories. Then he withdrew from the outskirts of Durazzo and led his army down into the rich plains of Thessaly, in Greece. Here his men would have plenty of food and they could rest while new plans were drawn up. The defeat at Durazzo had been humilating but no serious damage had been done to his fighting force. With slight reorganization it would soon be ready to engage in battle again.

Pompey, however, did not realize this. Misled and blinded by the opinions and advice of the senators who were with him in his camp, he decided that Caesar's army was completely wrecked and in full flight. Labienus also helped to deceive him. "Do not believe," he said, "that this is the same army which defeated the Gauls and Germans. I was in those battles and I know what I say is true. That army is no more. Part fell in action; part died of fever in Italy; many went home. The last veterans died here at Durazzo. What is left are only raw recruits from Cisalpine Gaul."

Pompey was no longer capable of thinking for himself, no longer commander of his army. The corrupt senators who were with him held sessions and debates, voting resolutions just as if they were still in the Senate in Rome! They decided on military tactics and expected Pompey to obey them. They had never liked Pompey; they had only won him over that he might serve them as a tool against Caesar. And they were now in no mood to listen to him.

They told Pompey that a single blow would now finish Caesar's army, that his men were obviously worn out and without spirit. And so sure were they of victory that they drew up elaborate plans for the future. They planned to kill Caesar and all his soldiers after the next battle. Then they would return in glory to Italy where they would set up a Senatorial Court in which all persons who had not openly supported them would be tried and sentenced. Everyone who had supported Caesar was to be killed at once, his property confiscated. And even those who had supported Pompey were not to escape! Any of Pompey's followers who had not taken an active part in the war were to be tried and punished according to the degree of their negligence. Cicero fitted into this last group and he now began to feel uncomfortable and longed once more to switch sides and rejoin Caesar.

The senators went even further than this. They fought among themselves as to whom should succeed Caesar as Pontifiex Maximus and get his palace and gardens in Rome!

And so it was that Pompey broke camp at Durazzo and followed Caesar into the plains of Thessaly. So it was that the Battle of Pharsalia was fought, a battle that has gone down in history because it was here that the aristocrats of Rome fought in defense of their corrupt and outmoded beliefs. Senators and their sons whose theory it was to run the government for their own benefit, heirs of many of Rome's most ancient families, chiefs of the conservative political party—all fought on this field to preserve their reactionary principles. At Pharsalia they came face to face with those who believed in and followed the democratic ways first defended by the Gracchi and Marius.

The two armies faced each other ready for action. Pompey commanded a force more than twice as large as Caesar's and felt that victory would surely be his. But

Caesar, watching Pompey's battle preparations from a hilltop, was quick to see through Pompey's scheme, and made his plans accordingly.

When all was ready he addressed his troops. He reminded them of the cause for which they were fighting and of how again and again he had tried to bring about peace and of how Pompey had refused all his offers. Then he ordered a trumpet to sound for the attack.

At that moment an old captain of his favorite Tenth Legion, one who had been with Caesar in Germany, Gaul, Britain and Spain, called out, "Follow me, my comrades! Strike and strike home, for your general. This is one battle that remains to be fought—and he will have his rights, we our liberty. General," he added, looking at Caesar, "I shall earn your thanks this day, dead or alive!"

Caesar's first line then moved forward, threw their javelins, then drew their swords and set upon the enemy. His next two lines and his cavalry came forward. Pompey's cavalry bore down and his outer forces closed in on the field, feeling certain that by this encircling movement they would end the battle.

But Pompey and his men did not know that Caesar had a fourth line hidden in reserve. And when they heard the trumpet sound and saw this fresh force suddenly appear on the field they became confused, gripped by fear. They tried for a while to hold the field but since the best cavalry is no match for well-armed infantry in close formation, they were forced to give way. Many were slain and the rest fled into the neighboring hills and woods.

Pompey also deserted the battle. He left the field and hid in his tent. From this opening skirmish he guessed only too well what the final result of the battle would be. He was no longer the great general and man he had once been. He had lost his self-respect, exchanged his honor for promises of glory. He was a complete victim of the corrupt senators to whose golden words he had foolishly listened. And during the rest of that day he received news of the battle from others who, like him, were no longer able to remain on the field.

By midafternoon the issue was settled. Caesar had won and the senatorial army was completely vanquished; twenty-four thousand men surrendered and fifteen thousand lay dead upon the field; one hundred eighty standards had been captured and all of Pompey's eagles. And among the dead were the bodies of many Roman senators and aristocrats.

"They would have it so," Caesar said sadly as he looked at their bodies dressed in the familiar Roman toga. "After all that I had done for my country, I would have been condemned by them as a criminal if I had not appealed to my army."

Then entering Pompey's deserted camp, he looked upon a strange scene. The tents of the Roman aristocrats had freshly laid turf floors and adjoining arbors over which were trained ivy and other vines. Here were couches on which the nobles could lounge, sheltered from the hot summer sun. There were also tables laid with silver plate and all sorts of choice wines and Roman delicacies. Everything was awaiting the return of the victorious aristocrats.

Caesar studied this unbelievable scene and then said, "These were the men who so falsely accused my troops of vice and degeneracy!"

Caesar had won the battle of Pharsalia, but Pompey, Labienus and several other officers had escaped. Pompey, who only a year before had proudly called himself "the first citizen of Rome," was now a fugitive. And in his tent was found his private correspondence revealing his long intrigues against Caesar and implicating him with many corrupt and prominent people of Rome. But Caesar refused to look through these letters. He wanted no revenge. He wanted the past to be forgotten. And so he burnt all these papers without reading them.

Caesar sought no revenge, inflicted no cruelty. And when Pompey's men surrendered he forgave them all without reserve. Many went down on their knees before Caesar and sobbed. But he bade them rise. He did not want them to humilate themselves. He spoke to them in simple, quiet words, trying to dispel their fears. He asked them only to promise not to bear arms against him again.

The battlefield of Pharsalia was strewn with dead. Most of these were followers of Pompey, but two hundred of Caesar's men and thirty centurions also lost their lives. Among these was the brave cenutrion of his famous Tenth Legion. Caesar ordered his men to search among the dead and bring his body out for special honors, special burial. They found the body and brought it away from the grim field as the light of the long day was closing upon them.

Caesar decorated his faithful dead centurion and ordered that he be given a funeral with full military honors. Caesar had not forgotten his words: "I shall earn your thanks this day, dead or alive."

Thus ended the great Battle of Pharsalia.

chapter
thirteen

POMPEY had fled.

When the Battle of Pharsalia was nearing its end, he mounted his horse and rushed out of the rear gate of his camp. He dashed from the sight and sound of his defeat and, riding at full fury, headed toward the eastern coast of Greece. On the way he was joined by a small group of his cavalry that had also taken flight. Together they rode day and night over the Grecian hills till they came to the Aegean coast. There they boarded a ship and set sail for the island of Mytilene off the coast of Asia Minor. It was here that Pompey's wife and young sons awaited him.

The inhabitants of the island had heard through false rumors that Caesar had been defeated and had bowed his head before Pompey's rage. And so they welcomed the "victorious" general. But when they learned the truth from Pompey's own lips, he and his family were no longer welcome and were forced to leave Mytilene at once.

Pompey sailed southward along the Aegean coast of Asia Minor to Cilicia, the scene of his pirate wars. Since this was one of the lands of his past glories, he felt certain that here he would find friends. But wherever he landed and sought refuge he was repulsed. The news of his defeat was already known and the people did not care to have him in their midst. Even the islands of Rhodes and Cyprus were embarrassed by his presence and so he was forced to sail on. He wanted to go to Syria but he was warned that he would not even be allowed to land on its shores, for the Roman governor of that province had just sworn allegiance to Caesar.

These were all lands which Pompey had once conquered, lands where his name had once been spoken of in awe. But now that he had fallen, in all this vast territory there was not one spot where he could find shelter and peace.

And so Pompey turned his eyes toward Egypt. Had he not always been friendly with the Egyptians? Had he not, years before, left a garrison of his soldiers behind in Alexandria as a token of his esteem for Ptolemy, the old king? It was true that old Ptolemy was now dead and his throne left jointly to his sixteen-year-old daughter Cleopatra and her younger brother; but these young people would certainly not forget their father's friend and would give him and his family refuge. Besides, the members of the Roman garrison could not possibly have forgotten their former general! This was the way Pompey reasoned. And so he sailed toward Egypt, together with his family and some two thousand troops he had collected on the way.

But Pompey did not know he was going toward the one land which was least disposed to welcome him. Egypt was, at that moment, torn by revolution. Young Ptolemy had stolen the throne from his sister Cleopatra, making himself king, while she had been forced to flee. The Roman garrison in Alexandria, many of whom had married Egyptian women, had just sworn allegiance to him. And with the news of the defeat of Pompey at Pharsalia, the Egyptians had decided that Rome, now torn asunder by civil war, was no longer to be feared.

So when Pompey's ships touched the Egyptian coast and he sent an envoy ashore asking for permission to land, the young king and his crafty guardians were not well disposed toward him. Pompey, more than any other man, symbolized to them the brute force of Rome. Besides, Caesar was now master of the great Empire. So while they plotted against Pompey, they pretended friendliness and gave him permission to land. They even sent a boat with special representatives to carry him ashore.

Pompey's wife distrusted the whole affair and begged her husband not to go. But Pompey brushed her fears aside. His pride would not allow him to believe that the Egyptians and his former Roman soldiers did not respect and love him. And so he stepped into the boat and started toward shore. But when he was only a short distance off, still within sight of his wife and young sons, he was brutally murdered. His head was cut off and carried away, his body thrown upon the sandy beach.

Now it happened by odd chance that a man, who had

once been Pompey's slave and had been set free by him, was living close by. And hearing of this act of treachery he searched for the headless body of his old master. Finding it he built a funeral pyre of driftwood and twigs and burned it there on the beach. Thus ended Pompey, an honest man but one who allowed pride to dictate to reason. In the flames of a pyre on the lonely coast of Egypt, far from his native Rome, a man who had once been master of millions left this world mourned only by one who had once been his slave.

Now during all these days, while Pompey wandered about seeking refuge, Caesar followed along his track hoping to overtake him. He feared that Pompey might manage to raise another army in the East and continue the bloodly Civil War. And he hoped to meet with him and come to some agreement. Perhaps Pompey could now be persuaded to come back to Rome as his friend.

Caesar followed Pompey to Egypt with a small force of three thousand men. And it was very fortunate that he had these soldiers with him, for shortly after arriving at Alexandria he and the Egyptians quarreled.

Hoping to please Caesar, the Egyptians presented him with Pompey's gory head. He was shocked and revolted by the sight and did not hide his feelings. He considered their act one of treachery. The Egyptians at once sensed that they had lost whatever respect Caesar might have had for them, and they gave vent to their true feelings. Mobs gathered in the streets and wherever Caesar appeared they shouted that Egypt was a free country, that their king should no longer be insulted by being forced to tolerate Roman troops in his land.

Caesar was very anxious to return to Rome, because

he knew that there were many pressing problems which needed his attention, but he did not feel that he could leave Egypt aflame with such anti-Roman feelings.

Sensing that open violence would soon break out, Caesar at once sent to Cilicia for troops. Then assuming a dictatorial manner he ordered that Ptolemy's will be observed and Cleopatra brought back to the throne. The citizens of Alexandria rose in anger at his words, deeply resenting Roman interference in their national affairs. Having made an end of Pompey they now decided to rid themselves of Caesar. He was in their hands. And so they secretly brought a large force of troops into the city and walled up Caesar and his three thousand soldiers in the royal palace and that part of the city adjoining the harbor.

However, having allowed himself to be trapped in this ridiculous manner did not seem to shake Caesar's faith in his power to fight his way out. He at once set fire to the docks and the Egyptian ships which were within his reach and fortified the palace and surrounding buildings. In this position he held off the entire Egyptian force for several months until his reinforcement finally arrived.

The Roman army from Cilicia, which had marched across Syria, at last entered Egypt. It captured a city at the mouth of the Nile, then hurried up the river toward Cairo. The Alexandrians immediately set out in pursuit. Caesar now saw his chance. He loaded his forces onto his ships and stole out into the Mediterranean, then sailed up the Nile to join his army of reinforcements near Cairo. Acting with his usual speed, he was waiting for the Alexandrians when they arrived. A battle

followed in which the Egyptian forces were completely
cut to pieces and young Ptolemy drowned in the Nile.

Alexandria now surrendered and Rome became complete master of all Egypt. Then Caesar at once recalled
Cleopatra and placed her on the throne. It was in this
way that the famous and beautiful Cleopatra became
queen of Egypt.

There are many romantic stories and legends about
Caesar and Cleopatra. Some tell of a journey they made
up the Nile in one of Cleopatra's luxurious barges.
Caesar, it seems, weary of long wars, foreign lands and
hard-won victories, welcomed the attentions which he
received. He rested under silken awnings while the gal-
ley slaves rowed the barge and the beautiful Cleopatra
and the ladies of her court played music and sang to him.

But these tales are not confirmed by history. While
Caesar was supposed to have been enjoying a life of
luxury with Cleopatra, he was actually being besieged
in Alexandria! And as soon as he escaped from this trap
and defeated the Egyptian army, he was forced to rush
to Asia Minor where revolts had broken out in the very
lands where he had, many years before, first served in
the Roman army.

Encouraged by the news that Caesar was trapped in
Egypt, a certain young noble had raised an army and
was leading it through Rome's eastern provinces, planning to liberate the people of these lands from the
Roman yoke.

Caesar and his troops, landing in Syria, at once
started inland to meet the army of this young noble and
put an end to his dream. This was Caesar's main object,
but as he traveled inland he also took time to attend to

political and diplomatic matters. He studied and reorganized the different provincial governments and cemented their bonds with Rome, trying to win as many friends as he could. He graciously received many rulers and chieftains, and because of his tact and wisdom and the rewards which he distributed, they all left him pleased and satisfied that he was their friend.

In time Caesar found the young noble and his army in a mountainous region close by the southeastern shore of the Black Sea. He tried to engage him in battle, but the young man, hoping to gain time, made overtures of peace. Caesar, however, quickly understood the treachery which was planned. Besides, he wanted to make an example of this young noble; he did not want to leave Asia Minor while one man in the eastern provinces still nurtured the dream of freedom from Rome. And so Caesar forced the young noble and his army into a battle. They were slaughtered, the young noble killed.

And it was following this concluding battle that Caesar sent his famous message back to troubled Rome, *"Veni, vidi, vici,—*I came, I saw, I conquered."

chapter
fourteen

CAESAR FELT that the Civil War should have come to an end with the Battle of Pharsalia. And in all fairness to the senatorial class, it must be said that many of them also shared this opinion and refused to continue open opposition.

However, there were others who were determined to fight on even if it meant the complete distruction of the Empire. And so while Caesar was busy stamping out the rebellion in Asia Minor, these men, some of whom had been leaders of the Senate and officers in Pompey's army, gathered in North Africa. They commanded Pompey's fleet and sixty thousand soldiers. Two of Pompey's sons by an early marriage and Labienus, Caesar's traitorous officer, were with them. They formed an alliance with King Juba, a dark-skinned native ruler of some North African lands. In return for his support and military aid they actually promised to give him the whole of Roman Africa!

This news reached Caesar before he left Asia Minor. And although he longed for peace, he knew that this threat would have to be eliminated. But the civil problems of Rome were so pressing that he dared not neglect them any longer. He had received urgent messages asking for his return. It seemed that since he had been elected consul for the second time, no new elections had been held. Three years had since passed. The government and the people looked upon him as the only person who was capable of directing the state; he was considered as perpetual annual consul or dictator.

Arriving in Rome, Caesar at once set to work. He attempted to restore financial stability by passing regulations aimed at restoring credit. Debtors were called upon to pay their obligations and securities were reassessed. The Senate was reorganized into a working unit. Men of ability were appointed to public offices and new governors chosen for the provinces. Money lenders were controlled but at the same time protected. To ease their lot, the poor were allowed free rent for a year. And minority groups, such as the Jews, were allowed freedom of worship and other privileges. The war veterans were given lands acquired from public properties and from some of Caesar's own private estates, each soldier also being given bonds and money which totaled seven hundred and fifty dollars.

In one way only did Caesar disappoint the people; he did not avenge himself and his supporters for the sufferings and abuses they had endured at the hands of Pompey and his friends. Caesar refused to punish even one of his political enemies. He killed no one, nor did he confiscate anyone's property. With his usual generosity he forgave all.

Because Pompey's followers had gathered a menacing force in North Africa, Caesar allowed himself only three months in Rome. At the end of this time he and his famous legions again embarked on a far-flung campaign.

Arriving in North Africa they at once engaged the senatorial forces and in the months that followed, although they fought with their characteristic bravery, they lost many battles and suffered many hardships.

And Labienus, as he had done before, mocked Caesar's soldiers. One day he rode up to a group that was being mercilessly pounded by his men and tauntingly asked them who they were and what they were seeking. An old soldier of the famous Tenth Legion answered him. He lifted up his helmet so that his former general could see his face, then hurled his javelin. It killed Labienus' horse.

The fighting was hard and Caesar's men were frightened on the battlefield by the enemy's elephants. But in spite of everything, the senatorial forces began to weaken on both sea and land. Caesar's ships drove Pompey's old fleet from the sea and the senatorial army suffered a sudden reverse because of a diplomatic error. Great numbers of soldiers of the senatorial forces deserted their ranks and poured into Caesar's camp because King Juba was being given precedence and their commander-in-chief had publicly exchanged his Roman imperial purple robe for a plain white tunic in the King's presence. These debasing acts so shocked and humilated the soldiers that they would no longer serve the senatorial cause.

As Romans, Caesar's men were also deeply mortified by these acts and they were now moved to fight more fiercely than ever. Even Caesar seems to have felt that his enemies had gone too far and that the time for clemency was over. And in the days that followed, some of the officers who were captured, men who had fought him in the Senate in Rome, in Spain and at Pharsalia, men whom he had repeatedly forgiven, were executed.

The last battle in North Africa was fought on a day in late spring. From a high hill Caesar and his forces happened to sight King Juba and the senatorial army busily building entrenchments for a camp. Caesar watched them calmly but his soldiers were gripped with an irresistible desire to attack at once. And Caesar, knowing the value of passion in battle, gave his consent. He jumped to his horse and led the charge. There was no real fighting. The senatorial army was thrown into complete panic. The elephants turned around and plunged into the midst of the men, trumpeting and roaring. Many were trampled to death and those who survived were slaughtered. No mercy was shown. Every man that was overtaken was killed. Some officers, however, escaped. They scattered in every direction, hoping to make their way to Spain. But only Labienus and Pompey's two sons managed to reach its shores. All the others were captured. Some committed suicide and the rest were executed. King Juba found his way to one of his country houses some distance away and threw himself upon his sword.

So ended the campaign in North Africa. And everyone believed that with this last battle the Civil War had been brought to a close. All of the senatorial army's main generals and leaders were now dead—all except Labienus.

But Labienus knew that Caesar would never forgive him and so he determined to make one last desperate stand. Arriving in Spain he fanned the embers of revolt, and together with a few other fanatics who straggled in from North Africa he managed to build up a force which again threatened Rome.

In the meantime Caesar returned to Rome once more to take up the problems of reform and reorganization. But the people were not satisfied to let their great hero begin work without first honoring him.

Caesar was officially proclaimed dictator for ten years with the right of nominating men of his own choice for the people to vote upon as consuls and praetors. And then four days were set aside for celebrations. There were triumphal processions and spectacles in the arenas. Sham naval battles were fought on artificial lakes. There were chariot races, animal slaughters and many bloody gladiator shows. Then Vercingetorix, the most noble of all the Gauls, was paraded in chains besides Caesar's chariot and later strangled in the dungeon of the Temple of Jupiter while the great conqueror offered his thanks at the altar above.

At last the people had their fill of rejoicing and Caesar was able to settle down to work.

He at once reorganized the Senate, expelling every member who was guilty of bribery or other corruption. And following his belief that conquered people should have a voice in the government at Rome, he filled the vacancies with men of merit and good character from all parts of the Empire. Some were Romans who had settled abroad but others were natives of conquered lands, including Gaul. He cleansed the law courts. Severe regulations were passed to outlaw the bribing of judges and other legal officers. His "Julian Laws," which had been passed many years before when he was consul for the first time, were now rigidly enforced. He proclaimed a general amnesty for all who had borne arms against him. By social laws he tried to lift the moral standard of the people, which had fallen to a very low state because of the demoralizing effect of the Civil War and the lack of a forceful government. He was named inspector of public morals. Crimes such as murder, abandonment of children by their parents, adultry, bribery and theft were widespread and Caesar tried to control them.

These reforms were all important to the welfare of the Roman state and Empire as it existed at the time. However, a certain reform which Caesar instituted at this period has continued to govern the lives of all the peoples of the Western world, from that time to this very day. Caesar ordered the revision of the Roman calendar, and it is because of this that our year is divided into twelve months, and approximately three hundred and sixty-five days of twenty-four hours each.

The Roman calendar of Caesar's day was constituted in the following manner. Twelve lunar moons fixed the number of months in the year. The number of days required to bring this lunar year to correspond with the sun was regulated by the members of the Sacred College. But since these men were not too interested in their work or too accurate in their calculations, during the century preceding Caesar the lunar year had advanced sixty-five days ahead of the sun. The "winter months" now came in the fall of the year, the "spring" in the winter.

Caesar decided to bring order out of chaos. He brought to Rome a man named Sosigenes, an Alexandrian astronomer, and asked him to supervise the reform of the calendar. It is probable that Caesar met this scholar while he was fighting in Egypt, and it shows that his interests were such that even during war he found time to study and associate with men of learning.

Sosigenes abandoned the moon as the basis for the calendar and based his new system on the sun. He had noted that the annual course of the sun was completed in three hundred and sixty-five days and six hours. And with this in mind he devised the calendar we live by today. He retained the twelve lunar moons to fix the number of months in the year, and adjusted the number of days in each month in order to use up the three hundred and sixty-five solar days. The extra hours were allowed to accumulate and every fourth year an extra day—the twenty-ninth of February—was added to the calendar. This fourth year is what we call leap year.

Sosigenes had planned that his new system should begin with the winter solstice. But for some reason Caesar preferred to have it start on the first new moon which followed. It happened that in 45 B.C., the new moon occurred eight days after the solstice and so the year started on the first of January. And thus it continues even to our time, two thousand years later.

Caesar did not accomplish the reform of the Roman calendar without suffering much criticism and ridicule.

He was a man of great intelligence and had been born before his time. He had vision while those around him were blind. And like all men who blaze new paths, he was laughed at by those who were incapable of understanding what was so obvious to him. Even Cicero, his boyhood friend, was one of those who mocked him. He said that Caesar was not content with the earth, he now wanted to be master of the sky. "The heavenly constellations," he remarked, "must now bow to Caesar's wishes!"

It was during this time, while Caesar was busy with the government in Rome, that disturbing news arrived from Spain. Labienus had succeeded in fanning the embers of revolt into a dangerous fire. With the aid of Pompey's sons, he was now heading thirteen legions made up of a strange mixture of people: Roman settlers, Moors, pirates and buccaneers, ragged remnants from the African campaign, veterans from Pompey's legions of former days and outlawed adventurers. It was to this low state that the haughty and corrupt senatorial forces had finally sunk. The cause of the aristocrats was now stripped of all its pretended dignity!

Caesar was reluctant to leave Rome and launch on still another campaign, but he knew that these bandits must be wiped out if there were to be peace.

Caesar was fifty-five years old and his health was beginning to fail. He realized he had only a few years left to live and would have preferred spending them in building a strong government for the Empire instead of fighting Labienus and his sorry legions. But since he knew he was the only one who could attend to this matter, he and his legions started out for Spain.

On this trip he was accompanied by a young man of

sixteen named Octavius, who was his sister's grandson, and Decimus Brutus, the officer who had served him so faithfully and with such distinction during the years and had commanded his fleet against the Veneti at Quiberon. These two men were closely associated with Caesar. Since Caesar was childless and had always wanted an heir, he decided to adopt Octavius legally. And only a few days before, he had designated Decimus Brutus as the future governor of Cisalpine Gaul.

Caesar and his forces arrived in Spain during the winter. And from the very first they were at a disadvantage. The weather was against them and they were forced to fight an enemy that had securely fortified itself behind the walls of the many Spanish towns and cities. However, the senatorial forces were drawn out on several occasions. Each time the battles were furious and no quarter was given by either side. Labienus and Pompey's sons knew that this was their last stand; it meant life or death. And Caesar's men, tired of war and impatient of Caesar's clemency toward the enemy, were determined that this time none would escape to fight them again.

The final battle of the Civil War took place on a plain which surrounded a little town called Munda. This place was situated close to the city of Cordova in south central Spain. The date was the seventeenth of March 45 B.C.

The Battle of Munda is known as one of the fiercest and bloodiest in all history. Its effect upon the Romans of that time was such that for several generations it was surrounded with legends. It was said that during that day holy images sweated, meteors streaked across the sky and the spirits of those long dead appeared upon the earth. But even more significant—the golden eagles carried by the senatorial legions suddenly took flight and crossed the battlefield to join those of Caesar's army! However these were only fanciful stories. The truth was quite different. The two armies were almost equal in number and fought with a desperation such as Caesar had never seen before. The entire battle was fought hand to hand with short swords, and so equal was the struggle that at one point Caesar jumped from his horse and, snatching a standard, tried to force his men to superhuman efforts in order to break the balance. But Caesar's attempt was not successful; the men could give no more. The battle was finally won by his forces, however, because of a strange accident. Labienus, curious about the action of some of his troops at the far end of the field, galloped off in full sight of all to see what was going on. Seeing this, his men were suddenly filled with terror. "He is fleeing! He is fleeing!" they cried. In another moment the senatorial forces were in full panic.

Some rushed toward the city of Cordova and managed to get behind its protecting walls before the gates were shut. Others dashed toward Munda. A few got into the town. The rest ran headlong against its walls and fell, a helpless mass, into the surrounding moat where Caesar's men slaughtered them. Among them was Labienus.

The defeat of the senatorial army was now complete. And such was the temper of Caesar's men that they were not satisfied simply to surround the city and town and wait. They stormed Cordova and massacred twenty-two thousand people, many of whom were innocent residents of the city. Then they went out onto the battlefield and, pinning together with javelins the bodies of the dead, they built a wall of corpses to surround Munda. Along the top of the wall they placed a line of heads— all facing inward toward the miserable trapped people. Those who were within then began to fight among themselves and in the end, completely devoid of hope, they surrendered.

In this gruesome way did the Civil War finally come to an end—a war which had been brought upon the whole Roman Empire by a small group of corrupt aristocrats of the senatorial class, in order to avoid simple and necessary reforms which they knew Caesar would pass if he became consul for a second time. Because of stupidy, selfishness and lack of vision these men had thrown their country into a bloody conflict. Their behavior stands to this day as a completely shameful thing.

The Civil War was now ended, the Empire secure. From the Gibraltar and the Atlantic to Persia, from the warm coasts of the Aegean and the Mediterranean to the cold shores of the North Sea, all was at peace. The military forces of the senatorial group had been completely defeated.

Now that hostilities were over, Caesar hoped all warring groups could learn to respect each other and cooperate for the good of the Empire. And with this firm belief he started back toward Rome. But he was wrong. Many hostile aristocrats awaited him. He had but six months longer to live.

chapter fifteen

BACK IN ROME once more, Caesar returned to his task of reform and reorganization which had been interrupted on three different occasions.

His first act was to try to erase every trace of animosity and fear which the aristocrats still felt against him and his followers. He knew they all hated him and he tried to bring them to a more reasonable opinion. He forgave even his most bitter enemies and restored properties and honors to the widows and children of those who had been killed in the war. Without partiality he appointed to high office any among the aristocrats who were capable and deserving. This included several men who had fought him openly. One was a former senator who had asked that Caesar be recalled from Gaul; another was a man who had publicly flogged a free citizen from Cisalpine Gaul and then sent him home to tell his fellow men what true Romans thought of Caesar. A third was a man who had plotted his death in Asia

Minor; a fourth one who had betrayed him in Egypt. And in the name of the united Empire he restored the statues of his great enemies Sulla and Pompey. The mob had overthrown them during the Civil War and now Caesar rededicated them with public ceremonies.

Satisfied that the effects of his generosity toward his enemies would in time destroy their hatred and win their friendship, he then turned to matters of government.

He increased the number of senators to nine hundred, creating new seats for representatives from all the provinces. He also admitted *libertini,* the sons of former slaves, who had risen to prominence through their own intelligence and ability. To maintain the free population in Italy he ordered all landowners and farmers to employ a certain number of free laborers in addition to their slaves. He did away with the grain dole in the city and settled the numberless poor on lands in Italy and abroad. From these homeless and unemployed people of Rome he organized groups of colonists which he sent out to distant parts of the Empire. They founded colonies in Gaul, Africa and Spain. It was some of these colonists who rebuilt Corinth and Carthage. Caesar also included his soldiers in this colonization program.

As inspector of public morals he tried to check the spread of luxury which was destroying the fiber of Roman character. Setting an example by his own simple and modest habits, he passed regulations to curb the excesses of the rich. Young and able-bodied patricians could no longer be carried through the streets of Rome in litters borne on the shoulders of slaves. Exotic foods and wines imported from the distant provinces could no longer be sold in the market places.

At this time Caesar also turned his attention to education and science. He founded libraries in many of the large cities and towns of Italy. He brought doctors and men of science to Rome from all parts of the Empire. He asked engineers to draw up plans for draining the marshes around Rome. For centuries these marshes had been the breeding grounds of malaria and other diseases, and had long impaired the health of the people. He ordered that the channel of the Tiber be changed and deepened and that new roads be built—not only in Italy but also in the provinces. And to help speed sea travel to the eastern provinces he conceived a plan of cutting a canal across the Isthmus of Corinth in Greece.

These are only a few of the many things which Caesar did after he returned from Spain. But he was worn out by long wars. His health was not good and he no longer worked with the strength and energy which he had shown in former times. He seemed to feel that his death was not far off, and was often heard to say that he had lived long enough. But in spite of this lowering of his spirit, he nevertheless began to make plans for one more campaign. After having spent so many long and exciting years in the army, he found life in Rome too restricting. Now that he had reformed the government he believed others could carry on the role of governing. And so he prepared to leave for the eastern frontier of the Empire which was being threatened.

This was the reason Caesar gave for wanting to leave Rome at this time, but there was still one more reason; his enemies and friends were heaping such honors upon him that he could no longer live as he chose—as a simple democratic leader. And he reasoned that while he was away in the East the fervor which his victories had kindled would cool.

During the months since Caesar's return from Spain he had been smothered with honors and distinctions. With the complete approval of the people, the Senate had voted him the title of "liberator." This title, together with his title of commander-in-chief, was to be hereditary in his family. Statues were erected in his honor in all parts of the city. Some were placed in temples, one on the Rostra—the speaker's terrace in the Forum—and another in the Capitol next to the statues of the Seven Kings of Rome. The day of his birth was declared a national holiday and the name of the fifth month of the year, Quintiis, was changed in his honor to Julius. To-day we call it July.

It seemed as though the Senate and the people of Rome could not do enough for their hero. They gave him a wreath of gold laurel leaves and robes of honor. In the Senate he had a golden chair, and he was presented with a golden chariot. A temple to Concord was ordered built to honor his generosity and forgiveness. His person was proclaimed sacred, and to injure him in any way was declared a sacrilege. Finally, when they ran out of honors and titles, the Senate declared that Caesar was not a man at all but truly a god or the son of a god. Was he not a descendant of Venus herself? And so a temple was ordered to be built in his honor, and Mark Antony, his devoted officer and friend, was named as priest.

Such were the honors which were heaped upon Caesar. And since he was a man of reason he became disturbed and uneasy. He felt that he must accept these gifts from the people or he would offend them. He knew the temper of the masses and the warmth of their enthusiasm. Had he not once been director of their great arena games? Yet he understood very clearly that if these flattering attentions continued he would become ridiculous in the eyes of all.

And he understood one thing more. He knew that his enemies had grasped at the enthusiasm of his friends in order to destroy him. It was clear to him that they had devised a sinister plan; they were encouraging his friends to heap new honors upon him and suggesting some on their own, with the sole purpose of raising him so high upon a pedestal that he would easily topple off!

His enemies, the aristocrats, looked upon every one of his reforms as a crime. They were still opposed to democratic ideas. They clung to the dead past and wanted to retain the old form of government. They deeply resented having to share the Senate with sons of slaves and representatives from the provinces. They did not believe in government by representation of those governed. They looked upon Caesar as one who had destroyed their profitable monopoly of power, not as one who had the vision to evaluate the needs of the present and future so that all might survive, rich and poor alike. And in their resentment these men sought any means of ridding themselves of Caesar. They would force him into a position from which he could not extricate himself or, if need be, they would drive a dagger into his heart.

Caesar understood only too well how his enemies felt about him. He had always been quick to sense the feelings of others. And besides, he had received reports of plots for his assassination. But he refused a bodyguard.

He was planning to leave Rome for the eastern campaign within a very short time; he believed that he could handle his enemies during these last few days. Then, once he was far from their sight, he thought they would forget their hatred of him. And so he continued living in his usual way. However, he tried to curb the attentions which continued to be heaped upon him. He refused to accept the role of a god and also declined a proposed ten-year consulship. And with his usual frankness he spoke openly of the plots against his life.

Hearing Caesar speak in this way, Cicero rose in the Senate to quell his fears. Cicero, who only a few years before had said that Caesar was but mortal and that "there are many ways in which a man can be got rid of," Cicero, whom Caesar had so often forgiven, now spoke false words of flattery and reassurance. He stood before the Senate and delivered a long speech that rang with fine phrases and high oratory. "Long have I been silent," he said, "not from fear but from grief. But the time for silence is now past."

Then with golden words he told how no general or king had ever before performed such exploits as Caesar. And turning toward Caesar and addressing him directly he continued, "You have conquered even yourself and restrained your resentment against your enemies and restored the civil rights of all. This deed raises you above humanity. . . . Justice, mercy, moderation, wisdom, all these traits in you we admire. . . . How can we praise, how can we love you sufficiently? By the gods, the very walls of this house are eloquent with gratitude. . . . No conqueror in a civil war was ever so mild as you have been. You have surpassed yourself. You have overcome victory in giving back the spoils to the conquered. By the laws of the war we were under your feet, to be destroyed if you so willed. We live by your goodness."

Then facing the Senate he said, "We were in arms against him, how impelled I know not. He cannot acquit us of mistake, but he holds us innocent of crime. . . . Me, of his own free will, he has restored to myself and to my country. . . . He has brought back the most illustrious survivors of the war. You see them gathered here in full assembly. He has not regarded them as enemies. He considers that you entered the war against him rather in ignorance and unfounded fear than from any motives of ambition or hostility. . . . I was always for peace. Caesar was for peace. Caesar's wars ended with the last battle. The sword is now sheathed."

Cicero then turned to another subject. He said that Caesar had lately expressed a fear of assassination. "By whom?" he asked boldly. "Not by his comrades, for they could not be so mad. And not by his enemies, for he has no enemies. But let us be watchful."

Then again he turned and addressed his words directly to Caesar. "Our lives are bound up in yours. . . . With sorrow I have heard you say that you have lived long enough. For glory perhaps you have. But for your country you have not. . . . Your great work is unfinished. . . . There can be no salvation for us unless you are preserved. Therefore, we exhort you, we beseech you to watch over your own safety. . . . From my own heart I say, and I speak for others as well as myself, we will stand as sentries over your safety. And we will interpose our own bodies between you and any danger which may menace you."

When these words were spoken the Senate rose as a body and each man present promised to protect Caesar with his life.

In this way Cicero tried to calm Caesar's fears of assassination while his friends, many of whom were in the Senate that day, continued with their dark schemes. They showered endless new honors on Caesar, even over his protests. Then one day they suggested that he should be king and his friends blindly and innocently supported this idea. They felt that he deserved this honor. Since he already had the power of a king, why should he not bear the title? Did not his statue already stand with the Seven Kings of Rome? Even the army was in favor of it. And so the Senate voted that Caesar should be king and they offered him a crown.

But Caesar sought no such position. He immediately refused the crown which was offered him. And if he had ever held any doubts about the temper of his enemies, he understood it now. He saw clearly through their plot. He knew that his enemies had suggested this high honor only to destroy him. The Roman people were very sensitive about titles. If Caesar had accepted the crown their hearts would at once have turned against him.

Caesar fully understood these things and did not hesitate to renounce the offer. But his enemies would not be put off so easily. They got someone to place a crown upon his statue in the Forum. It was done during a public celebration and while Caesar was present. But two of his friends — tribunes — immediately tore it down. Then a few days later, as he was riding through the streets of Rome, a crowd of people who had been led on by the aristocrats hailed him as king. Caesar stopped and denied the title.

After this one more attempt was made to force the kingship upon him. At another public celebration, as Caesar sat before a vast crowd of Romans in his purple robes of state, another crown was placed upon his head with these words, "The people give you this."

But Caesar removed the crown and called out in a loud voice for all to hear, "The Romans have no kings but their gods." And he ordered that the crown should be taken to the Capitol and placed upon the head of the great god Jupiter. The crowd burst into wild cheers; now they were sure that their idol would not betray them. And they had a brass tablet inscribed and put in a prominent place. It said that the Roman people had offered Caesar the crown and that he had refused it.

The aristocrats were now forced to admit that their plot had failed. But they were not willing to surrender. Caesar would be in Rome only a few days more. He was due to leave for the East just after the Ides of March (15th of March). Bitterness and hatred had blackened their hearts.

Murder was now on their lips.

With the stage thus set and at a given signal, the deed would then be accomplished. And after? They would rush into the streets proclaiming Caesar a tyrant. And his body would be thrown into the Tiber! His property would be confiscated!

Rumors of the plot were whispered about in Rome. But during the last few months there had been so many rumors of the same sort that no one paid much attention —not even Caesar. He continued to go about his daily affairs as usual, without a bodyguard.

However, on the morning of the Ides of March he became uneasy. His wife had heard that the sacrifices in the Temple were unfavorable and she had had a nightmare. "I saw your body covered with blood," she said, "and I was weeping over you." She begged him not to go to the Senate that day. And Caesar agreed to stay at home. But presently his trusted officer and friend Decimus Brutus came to get him. It was almost noon. He had been sent by his fellow conspirators; they were determined to carry out the deed on that particular day. Delay might be fatal to their plans.

It was not hard for Decimus Brutus to persuade Caesar to go with him. Caesar brushed away his wife's dream and the warnings of the Temple priests. "Should the Senate be dismissed because of a dream? Am I to be frightened because a sacrificial sheep is without a heart?"

However, before he left his home something else occurred which disturbed him. As he and Decimus Brutus passed down the hall toward the street door, his statue fell to the floor and broke. He stopped for a moment but then went on his way.

Once out in the city streets, he was warned twice more. A stranger handed him a scroll and begged him to read it at once. But Caesar believing it to be a petition, put it in among other scrolls he was carrying and walked on. The scroll contained a list of all the conspirators and a detailed account of the plot!

As Decimus Brutus and Caesar approached the Senate House, they were met by a soothsayer. This same man had warned Caesar a few days before. "Beware of the Ides of March," he had cried. And now on this day he repeated these same words. "Beware of the Ides of March!"

Caesar smiled at the old man and replied, "You see, the Ides have come and all is well."

"But they are not yet passed," answered the soothsayer.

Caesar now entered the Senate. Most of the senators were in their places, however; Mark Antony and another senator were standing at the door busily engaged in conversation. Caesar passed them and walked to the front of the chamber where he seated himself in his golden chair. At once, the conspirators rose and gathered about him, pretending friendliness. He did not suspect them. There was not one among them who did not owe him a personal debt of gratitude. They talked freely together. Some had favors to ask. Others had stories to tell.

A scroll was then placed in Caesar's hand and as he unrolled it and began to read its contents, his toga was suddenly grabbed and torn from his shoulders. He was stabbed in the throat by a dagger.

He rose to his feet with a cry and caught the arm of the one who had struck him. Then he was stabbed again by another. He looked around and saw that he was surrounded by a ring of daggers. There was no chance of escape. He lifted the folds of his toga over his head. The daggers struck him from every side.

The conspirators now drew back. Caesar reeled, took a few faltering steps and fell dead at the feet of Pompey's statue.

Cicero was present in the Senate. Although he had not taken part in the actual murder he was in full sympathy with the conspirators. And Brutus lifted his bloodstained dagger for Cicero to see and shouted, "Liberty is now restored!"

The stunned senators on the floor of the chamber now realized what had happened. With cries of horror they rose from their seats and in the wildest confusion ran from the building and out into the Forum. Mark Antony and some of Caesar's other close friends, being unarmed and fearing for their lives, ran with them.

"Caesar is dead!" they cried. "Murdered. Caesar is dead!"

These words were taken up by those in the Forum and passed on to others. Soon every street in Rome rang with the dismal cry, "Caesar is dead!"

The conspirators, however, were bold and they also went out into the Forum and the city streets crying, "The tyrant is dead! Rome is free!"

And there were some senators and others who joined the murderers. While they had had no part in the plot, now that the deed was done they wanted to share in its glory. At times like these there are always some who, having risked nothing, want to join a successful venture in the hope of gain. But through their foolishness and vanity, those who marched with the murderers on that day lived to regret their actions. They not only lost their honor but in a few days many also lost their lives.

Hearing the cries, the people of Rome were aghast. The entire population was stunned. They stopped in the streets and looked at each other. It seemed unbelievable. And then, suddenly, fearing that this violent deed might be a signal for an uprising—a bloody reign of terror— the tradesmen closed their shops and many ran to their homes and locked the doors.

Caesar's body lay deserted on the cold marble floor of the Senate. The statue of Pompey stood over him. All had fled, both friends and enemies.

Here in this very hall, only a few short weeks before, Cicero, the golden-tongued orator of Rome, had spoken words of praise and promise. "We live by your goodness. . . . There can be no salvation for us unless you are preserved. . . . From my own heart I say, and I speak for others as well as myself, we will interpose our own bodies between you and any danger which may menace you."

These words had echoed through the Senate chamber. And to this the senators had vowed. But now all was silent. All were gone, even Cicero. He had supported the murderers and now he took a share in the deed. "Is there any man," he asked, "who disapproves? All the good and wise joined in killing him. Some were not consulted, some wanted courage, some opportunity. But all were willing."

However, Cicero was wrong. There were many who disapproved. The people of Rome disapproved. In fear of Caesar's murderers they had rushed to their homes and hidden behind locked doors. But that did not signify their approval of the deed. All afternoon they dared not stir. The Forum and the streets were deserted and a strange silence hung over everything — an ominous silence. And the conspirators, who only the night before had spoken easily of how they would throw Caesar's dead body into the Tiber, did not even dare approach the Senate building. There was no one in the streets to stop them but they were suddenly filled with such fear that they could think only of hiding. They gathered in the Capitol and argued among themselves as to their next move. Cicero was with them.

Then later that afternoon, as the sun was setting, the people began to come out into the streets again. They wandered about aimlessly or stood about in silent groups. The entire population was too shocked to know what to do.

And it was during this time that three of Caesar's slaves entered the Senate building and lifted his body, bleeding from twenty-three dagger wounds, and carried it through the streets back to his palace. But even the sight of their dead idol did not raise the people from their stupor. Their grief was such that they could not speak, could not act.

Learning of this, the murderers in the Capitol, decided to act aboldly. Two of them came out into the streets and, gathering together several groups of the silent people, they addressed them. They spoke in defense of the old government and said that Caesar had overthrown the people's sacred rights. They talked of "liberty" and defended Caesar's assassination as an act of patriotism. They claimed to be innocent of private hatred, asserting they had acted only for the good of all.

But even though their words were eloquent they were not able to move their listeners. Again and again they tried to fan the sparks. But the fire would not kindle. The people just stared at them in cold, dead silence. At last they returned again to join their friends in the Capitol.

Although the people had listened to their words, they had not been deceived. They knew that these men were the very ones who only a short time before had showered Caesar with honors. These were the men who had tried to call him a god! These were the men who had tried to crown him king! Their treachery was now laid bare for all to see. And the people of Rome understood only too clearly what had happened.

It was true, they admitted, that Caesar had held power greater than any Roman had ever held before. But they could not see where this power had been abused. In their eyes Caesar had done only good for Rome. He had extended the Empire and welded it into a strong, working unit. He had given the people land and employment. Many now held citizenship. His good deeds were too numerous to count. He had always acted with generosity and humanity even toward his most bitter enemies. No, they could not take up the cry of "liberty." They could only look upon the ghastly deed with horror.

Night began to fall. A detachment of soldiers under one of Caesar's old officers entered the city and occupied the Forum. Some of the people lingered in the streets waiting for something, they knew not what. Others gathered in a great sorrowing crowd before Caesar's palace. And his murderers in the Capitol argued on among themselves.

All night Caesar's murderers sat and talked and schemed. They did not know which way to turn. They had miscalculated; their plans had gone astray. Those who had been so sure of themselves the night before were now full of doubts. They were certain that the public would hail them as liberators. But they had been unable to arouse the people. And now, with time to reflect, they suddenly realized that if Caesar were declared a tyrant, they would be destroyed. If Caesar were proclaimed a tyrant then all his laws and appointments would be null and void. And since most of these conspirators had been appointed to high office by Caesar, they would at one stroke lose their positions and their authority. They and their friends held governorships and other desirable posts through Caesar's appointments. Cicero and his son-in-law had been designated as consuls. These were not honors men cast lightly aside.

Besides, thousands of colonists, former legionnaires as well as ordinary citizens who had been promised lands, were waiting to set sail for their new homes. If these promises were now withdrawn one could easily imagine what would happen. Then, too, if Caesar were denounced and his body thrown into the Tiber like a common criminal, his army might rise in protest.

And so after hours and hours of deliberation the murderers determined to appeal to Caesar's friends to save them. They decided to ask Mark Antony to help them preserve the government. And Mark Antony being a sane man, one who could face accomplished facts, agreed to help call the Senate into session.

The Senate convened on that same day—the day following the murder—in one of the city temples; none of the senators cared to return to the Senate building. And Mark Antony presided as consul.

Cicero was the first to rise and speak. His purpose was to erase as much of the guilt as possible. He first briefly reviewed Roman history, speaking of the Gracchi, of Marius and Sulla, of Pompey and Caesar. He described the fate of Grecian cities such as Athens, cities which had been torn by opposing factions, and he warned that Rome would also fall if peace were not quickly established between the Senatorial and Popular parties. "Caesar is slain," he said. "The Capitol is held by the representatives of the Senate, the Forum by soldiers, and the people are filled with terror. Is violence to be answered by more violences? During these past few years we have lived . . . in cycles of recurring revenge. Let us now forget the past. Let us draw a veil over all that has been done, not looking too curiously into the acts of any man. . . . Let Caesar's ordinances and let Caesar's appointments be maintained. What is done cannot be undone."

In the interest of public peace, he suggested that Caesar be given a simple private burial. He warned that a public funeral might arouse the people unnecessarily. "At such trying moments as this," he said, "the welfare of the people must be given the greatest consideration."

With these fine words Cicero hoped to smooth over

the crime and pave the way for his fellow conspirators to retain the high posts to which Caesar had appointed them. He succeeded in part. The Senate voted an act of "oblivion" and so he and his friends were saved for the time being. But Caesar's murder could not be brushed aside quite so lightly.

Mark Antony was true to Caesar and had no intention of allowing his body to be quietly buried as though his life had been spent in crime and corruption. Besides, out in the city streets the people were beginning to question what had happened. And as they reviewed Caesar's life they became more and more fixed in their love for their dead leader. They felt he had spent his entire life defending them against the abuses of the aristocrats. It was he who had wiped away oppressors at home and abroad. It was he who had always fought for them. And they knew that it was because of this that he had been murdered. No Roman had ever served his country better in peace or war. And this was his reward!

And so the murderers and their friends in the Senate were forced to accept defeat concerning Caesar's burial. Mark Antony won his wish, and Caesar's body was brought from his palace to the Forum and placed upon the Rostra. His toga had not been changed. It was soaked with blood and torn by the thrusts of the daggers. The ghastly evidence was visible for all to see.

Mark Antony now stepped forward on the Rostra and faced the thousands who had gathered to mourn. In his hand he held Caesar's will. He broke the seals, opened the document and in a quiet but clear voice he began to read. A hush fell over the vast crowd.

If any present had ever questioned Caesar's love for

them, the very first words of his will erased all doubt. It reminded the Romans that they had always been first in his thoughts. Out of his vast wealth, Caesar left every citizen of Rome a small sum of money. Everyone, no matter how humble or lowly his station, became a benefactor. And the people also inherited part of his preperty; he left them his gardens on the Tiber as a public park and recreation ground.

As Mark Antony continued reading, the people learned that Caesar's adopted son, Octavius was to be his personal, military and political heir. And should Octavius die or fail as a ruler, then his place was to be taken by Decimus Brutus.

When the name Decimus Brutus was heard, a wave of emotion swept through the throng. Mark Antony paused. The people looked at one another as though to say, "This one he trusted. This one was second as his heir. And the hand that would have accepted the gift has struck Caesar down with a dagger!"

The words of Caesar's will bore proof of the love which he had felt for Decimus Brutus and of the trust he had placed in him—a love and trust which had been repaid by foul treachery. Mark Antony, sensing the mounting passion of the crowd and wanting the people to feel the full weight of the dark deed which had been committed by the aristocrats, stood silently before them holding Caesar's will aloft for all to see. The document spoke for itself. It gave full proof of the blackest betrayal.

In an effort to prove beyond all doubt how base and vile Caesar's enemies were, he asked a herald to step up and read a list of the extravagant honors which the Senate had recently heaped upon Caesar against his wishes, as well as the oath which each had sworn to personally defend Caesar from all harm.

When the last words of these past betrayals had been spoken by the herald, Mark Antony then moved over to Caesar's bloody body and began to speak. Quietly and simply, he spoke of Caesar's family, his birth, his boyhood, his simple way of life. He described his generous nature and his tolerance for his enemies, and how, being without evil himself, he was unwilling to believe evil of others.

"Power in most men," he said, "has brought their faults forward. Power in Caesar only displayed his excellence. Prosperity and fame did not make him insolent. Of his laws I could speak forever. His campaigns in Gaul are now part of Rome's glory. The German hordes who would have poured over the Alps are now quiet. Caesar might well have added Germany and Britain to our Empire, but his enemies would not have it so. They regarded the government as theirs. They continued to take more and more power into their hands. . . . Civil war brought him home, for it was you yourselves who needed his help. He set you free. He set Spain free. He labored for peace with Pompey, but Pompey preferred to flee to Greece and raise the eastern powers against you. And in the end Pompey perished. He died of his own obstinacy!"

Now Mark Antony's voice grew stronger. He felt the approval of the crowd and he gathered confidence.

"Caesar took no honor to himself for his victory over Pompey," he continued. "He took no revenge. He even praised those who had been faithful to Pompey. He was sorry for Pompey's death and treated his murderers as they deserved. He destroyed your enemies in Egypt and on the distant shores of the Black Sea. Then he restored order and peace in Africa and Spain, and again his one desire was to spare his fellow citizens. . . . All through all this he remained ever the same. He was never carried away by anger. He was never spoilt by success. He did not seek vengeance; he never tried to secure his future by violent deeds. He repaired old acts of injustice. He brought home those who were in exile and restored properties that had been confiscated. He burnt unread the correspondence of Pompey so that those who were mentioned and compromised might not suffer or fear injury. . . . You honored this man as your father. You made him chief of your nation; the most you had to give was less than he deserved. Toward the gods he was High Priest. To you he was Consul; to the army he was Imperator; to the enemies of his country, Dictator. In brief he was Father of His Country. And this your father, your Pontifex, this hero, this person whom the senators all vowed to defend with their lives, lies dead. Not by disease or age has he died. Not by war or the visitation of the Gods. But here at home, by conspiracy within your own walls, slain in the Senate hall where he went unarmed, not as a warrior but as a peacemaker, sitting in his seat of judgment, naked to his foes. He whom no foreign enemy could hurt has been killed by his fellow countrymen! He who so often showed mercy has been killed by those whom he had forgiven!"

Mark Antony now bowed his head and spoke to the corpse lying at his feet.

"Where, Caesar, is your love for mankind? Where is

the sacredness of your life? Where are your laws? Here
you lie murdered, here in the Forum, through which so
often you marched in triumph. Here on this very Rostra
from which you addressed your people. And now, alas,
your gray hairs are dyed with blood. You lie dressed in
a stained and torn toga. In this have you been robed for
the sacrifice!"

Line by line, Mark Antony's impassioned language
had taken effect. The people had been roused to fury.
They had been inflamed. They declared war against Caesar's murderers and their friends. They cursed the conspirators. They cursed the Senate. They could no longer
be held back. They surged toward the Rostra and lifted
Caesar's body aloft. The funeral was now in their hands.

Some wanted to carry Caesar's body to the Temple of
Jupiter in the Capitol and burn it before the very eyes of
his murderers. Others wanted to take it to the Senate and
cremate it at the very scene of the crime, using the Senate
chamber as a pyre. All began shouting at once and in the
confusion they did not know which way to go.

Then some soldiers, fearing that the burning of the
Senate might start a fire which would consume half of
Rome, suggested that Caesar's body should remain in the
Forum. They said that it was more fitting for the man
who had been the friend of the people to be cremated in
the Forum, the meeting place of the people, than to be
carried back into the building which through all these
years had sheltered the people's enemies, the aristocrats.

The crowd was impressed by these words and the
Rostra was at once torn apart and the boards and benches
piled into a great heap. Caesar's body was then placed
upon it and the fire was lit. And as the flames consumed

his body, the people came forward to add a tribute to the burning pyre. Each gave of what he had. Musicians threw their instruments into the flames, women their jewels, actors their costumes, soldiers their swords, children their toys.

The flames burned all night long. And soon Caesar, he who had been ruler of the whole civilized world, master of the Roman Empire, was no more. The great conqueror was now dust.

In the morning his ashes were lovingly collected and borne to the tomb of the Caesars in the Campus Marius outside the city wall. Here they were buried by the grieving crowd.

But with this the people's sorrowing did not cease. Day after day, night after night, great crowds collected in the Forum to lament. The Jews of Rome, to whom Caesar had given freedom of worship and shown great tolerance, were among these. There were also great numbers of freedmen and people from the provinces.

chapter
seventeen

THE PUBLIC demonstration of mourning which had taken place at Caesar's funeral came as a complete surprise to the murderers. They had believed they would be hailed as heroes; instead, they found that they were looked upon as traitors and common criminals. Their plot had been successful; they had forgotten only one thing, an important thing, the people. And now sensing the temper which was rising, they fled for their lives. Some hid in the country. Others escaped into the eastern and North African provinces. Here they planned to await developments.

Time, they believed, was on their side; with time the people would forget and they could safely return to Rome. They would then win Mark Antony over to their side. And Octavius, Caesar's heir, was only eighteen, completely inexperienced in the ways of life and could therefore be easily handled. However, the conspirators were soon to discover that they were also mistaken in these beliefs.

Young Octavius was with the army in Greece when the news of Caesar's death reached him. And when he learned that he had been appointed as Caesar's political and military heir, he swore to avenge his adopted father's death and to dedicate his life to enforcing the new government and way of life that Caesar had evolved for the Empire. He at once set out for Rome.

Here he found several gigantic tasks confronting him. Since he was unknown to the people, he had to win their confidence. He had to prove his ability to the army. He had to make peace with Mark Antony who, feeling that Caesar should have chosen him as his political and military heir, was jealous of him. And he had to cope with Cicero, who alone of all the conspirators had ventured back into Rome. With Caesar dead, Cicero considered himself the first citizen of Rome and he planned to become the supreme ruler. He came back and took up his position as consul and set about to win the Senate's backing.

These were not easy matters to solve but Octavius soon proved that he was more than equal for the position which he had inherited. Although he was young, he was a person of great intelligence and character. There was much of Caesar in him. No problem seemed too great for him to overcome. And when it was reported to him that Cicero had boasted that he would use him to destroy Mark Antony and then cast him aside, he answered, "Cicero will learn that I shall not be played with so easily."

And this was exactly what Cicero and a great many

other people came to learn. After one year of political confusion, Octavius managed to win over Mark Antony and the army. Then, leading some of Caesar's old legions down from Gaul, he entered Rome to punish Caesar's murderers and claim his inheritance as ruler.

Octavius and Mark Antony were not men who believed in clemency toward their enemies as Caesar had. They drew up a list of three hundred names of people whom they felt were enemies of the state. This list included Cicero and all his fellow conspirators as well as senators and others who had approved of Caesar's murder. A reward the equivalent of fifteen thousand dollars was offered for the head of each person listed. Caesar's murderers were to be rooted out. And to prevent those who were in Rome from escaping, all exits from the city were guarded.

Thus opened a reign of terror unequaled in Roman history. Soldiers went from home to home seeking out the guilty. Some hid in wells, in sewers, in chimneys and in attics. But they were found and killed. Some resisted and others, seeing they could not possibly escape, committed suicide. A few, who had been cruel masters, were murdered by their own slaves.

Cicero, who was at his country estate, boarded a ship and tried to escape to one of the provinces. But a fierce storm arose and the ship was forced back into port. His slaves who loved him urged him to start out again but he felt defeated and refused to leave. He said he preferred to await the soldiers. However, when the news came that Octavius' soldiers were close, his loyal slaves put him in a litter and started down toward the shore. But they were overtaken by the soldiers. The slaves were armed and wanted to resist, but Cicero ordered them to put down the litter and save themselves. They did not want to abandon him but when he insisted they reluctantly obeyed his last command.

When the soldiers arrived, Cicero thrust his head out between the curtains of the litter. In an instant it was struck off.

Cicero's head was then brought back to Rome and hung in the Forum. And the soldiers who had accomplished the deed were handsomely rewarded. They received the equivalent of one hundred fifty thousand dollars. Cicero's head was worth ten times the head of the other conspirators!

In this way did Cicero meet his end. His eloquence had a tremendous influence on his time. Rome had never before had such an orator. And Rome was never again to have his equal. His tongue was golden but his words were poisoned with insincerity. Now his head, hanging in the Forum, was silent.

The Terror continued. Octavius and Antony did not rest until the very last conspirator had paid with his life. Even those had had fled to the provinces were hounded and all met violent ends.

Octavius now took up the serious task of ruling. And in time he proved himself a true heir of Caesar. He was not as brilliant or glamorous as Caesar but he showed tremendous ability in dealing with his enemies and in governing the vast Empire. He won the hearts of his people completely. And seventeen years after Caesar's death he was crowned as the first emperor of Rome, taking the name Augustus. He promoted the arts and developed agriculture. He ushered in the golden age of Latin literature. But above all he remained true to his vow that he would enforce the new government and the new way of life which Caesar had brought about.

Caesar was dead but Octavius did everything in his power to keep his spirit alive. He understood what a great man Caesar had been and he dedicated his life to carrying forward the ideas which Caesar had envisioned.

Caesar had seen that the Roman state built within a walled city had burst its bonds. And he helped form a new society. He remodeled a government which served the few into a government which served the many. He rose above the prejudices of his class and recognized the rights of the people. His one purpose always was justice for all. With this as his goal, he remodeled the government of the Empire. And once his ideas were established the Empire flourished for two hundred years.

Through his deep sense of justice and humanity, Caesar became one of history's most profound statesmen. And time, long centuries of time, have not dimmed his greatness.

BIBLIOGRAPHY

Caesar: War Commentaries. Everyman's Library.

Suetonius: The Lives of the Twelve Caesars. Modern Library.

Plutarch's Lives: Modern Library.

Froude, James Anthony: Caesar. Charles Scribner's Sons. 1937.

Fowler, W. Warde: Julius Caesar. Putnam's Sons. 1891.

Thaddeus, Victor: Julius Caesar and The Grandeur that was Rome. Brentano's, 1929.

Durant, Will: Caesar and Christ. Simon and Schuster, 1944.

index

185